the gift book

PATRICIA DAVIDSON

Also by Patricia Davidson:

The Shopaholic's Guide to Buying Online
The Shopaholic's Guide to Buying Fashion and Beauty Online
The Shopaholic's Guide to Buying for Mother and Child Online
The Shopaholic's Guide to Buying Gorgeous Gifts Online
The Shopaholic's Guide to Buying Online 2008
The Shopaholic's Top 1000 Websites

All these titles are available from Capstone, a John Wiley company.

the *gift* book

PATRICIA DAVIDSON

'A gorgeous guide to perfect presents.'
IAIN BURTON
CHAIRMAN, ASPINAL OF LONDON

CAPSTONE

For
Andrew, Sholto, Calum and Kirstie

INTRODUCTION

*H*ave you ever received a present that makes you wonder if the giver actually knows you at all? Just think for a moment and be honest. If you're anything like me, the answer will be: lots of times.

If that sounds even remotely ungrateful – after all, it's surely wonderful to be given a gift – I'm afraid it's nonetheless true. We just don't, on the whole, put enough thought into who we're buying for – either because we've left it right up until the last minute, so we're in a mad flat panic, or because we just don't give it the time.

At this point don't let me have you thinking that I always get it right – I most definitely don't; and being married to a man who will always ask if something can be returned if he doesn't like it (he's a Scot), and with extremely vocal kids, I'm always left in no doubt at all when I've got it wrong. Having said that, last year at Christmas I scored an unheard of three out of four. Yes, the expensive, modern food processor for my (chef-inclined, 20-year-old) son did have to go back because he specifically wanted something else that he hadn't bothered to tell me about, but the Karen Millen leather jacket for my 17-year-old daughter, the Strabo SatNav for my 19-year-old newly driving son, and the first edition autobiography of Rudyard Kipling for my poetry-loving husband were all real hits. It felt really good, I can tell you.

Anyway, enough of all of that. I decided to write this book because, being something of a shopping expert (did I hear the word 'addict' being bandied about?) and having travelled the world in search of wonderful shops while others took in the culture at galleries and museums (and having discovered more incredible places to shop both online and offline than you might have had hot dinners), I thought that this would be a good time to get it all down on paper and turn the gift-finding part of your life into a breeze.

In the four sections following, you'll find gifts for all sorts of different occasions and people, and my fast-track formula for getting it all right. However, while I can make suggestions on what to buy for just about everyone, let's get real here; there are so many different types of people on this planet that I could never cover them all, nor do I want to try. The art is to change your way of thinking so that no matter who you are buying for, the ideal choice of gift pops into your head quickly, and with the minimum amount of effort. QED (I hope).

My family think I'm difficult to buy presents for, no matter how much I tell them I'm really not. So, kids, this year, just remember: a salon gift voucher, something cashmere (preferably black), and anything in my favourite fragrance by Chanel. No pink fluffy dice. No silly books. Sorted. Thank you.

NOTE
All the entries are alphabetised within their sections by website name. Those beginning with 'the' appear under 'T'.

WHAT MAKES A PRESENT PERFECT?

*C*hoosing the right gift for the right person is an art. It should be a fun, pleasurable art – but in reality it's not that simple; if it were, we'd be spot on and get it right every time.

Think how often, throughout the year, you spend time buying cards and gifts for family, friends, kids and colleagues, exhausting yourself, as you try to find that perfect present, that special something that will make your gift a little bit different. We should all be present-buying experts; after all, we buy for birthdays, anniversaries, weddings, mother's day, father's day, Valentine's day and other occasions when we want to say 'thank you' and 'congratulations', not forgetting that monster of gift-giving occasions – Christmas.

Think about yourself for a moment. Which presents have been the best you've ever received, other than ones that you've sent loud and clear hints about, such as (in my case) salon gift vouchers, a particular brand of cosmetics, and a treadmill? (Yes, I did hint about that diamond from Tiffany, but it hasn't come my way – yet. I live in hope.) Who's actually got it right with you and why? What made it right?

You have to admit that the gifts that are spot on are almost always from people who know you well or who have gone to some trouble to find out about you. Yes, luck can play a part, but only very occasionally. The hastily bought and thoughtless gift usually sticks out a mile.

In order to choose perfect presents you need to spend a bit of time thinking about your recipient, and the best way to do this is to create a profile that you'll use every time for that person.

This relates to personal outlook, style, lifestyle, homestyle, interests, likes and dislikes.

OUTLOOK

Young or old? It doesn't so much matter what a person's actual age is as whether they're 30 going on 60, or the other way round. People always fall into one category or the other. Just consider some of the people you know and you'll see that I'm right. If you're buying for someone who is young in outlook, you can be a bit more adventurous about what you buy.

I'll give you an example. My 87-year-old mother-in-law still travels the world teaching Ikebana (Japanese flower arranging). She has schools in the USA, Germany and Holland, and has the equivalent of a black belt in the art. Young in years? Certainly not. Young at heart? Without question. You will know instinctively whether someone is young or old in outlook, and it's one of the first things you need to recognise.

PERSONAL STYLE

Is the individual's personal style classic or contemporary? Is he or she bohemian, minimal, sporty, luxe-loving or an adventurous dresser? If female, does she wear huge dangly earrings or neat little studs? Loads of colour or mainly neutrals? Does she always wear bright red lipstick or never use lipstick at all? Ridiculously high heels or flat shoes? This information all comes together tell you what you need to know.

Favourite colours are important and, just as important, are the colours you never see that person wearing. Noticing the latter will steer you clearly away from any clothing and accessory disasters. If the person always wear black or neutrals, don't go spending your money on a bright blue pashmina – you can bet she won't use it, even if you think she should. Just don't go there, you'll be wasting your money, I can promise you.

I have friends who wear chic (as opposed to scruffy) jeans all the time, and friends who wouldn't be seen dead in a pair; those for whom Issey Miyake's Pleats Please is wonderful and modern, and those who would prefer to wear a long skirt and boots. I have friends who always make the latest look seem fresh and easy, and those who wouldn't be bothered even to try. Why am I talking so much about clothes here? Because if you recognise someone's style, it almost always spills over into everything they do and what they like to have around them.

In part two, The Gift Lists, I will introduce you to some typical characters you might need to buy gifts for. In my family I have a Boy Racer/Kitchen Genius who dresses very tradition-ally and should never do anything else. I also have an Adven-turer/Kitchen Genius/Gadgetman (yes, lucky me), who again dresses traditionally (with modern touches). There is also a wannabee Boy Racer/Sporting Genius, who's much more ur-ban in style, and a Pampered Princess/Dancing Queen. If you know me, I'm sure you can guess who they all are.

So consider the following categories of personal style and then create your own descriptions:

Fashion forward ✿ Classic casual (preppy) ✿ Contemporary ✿ Traditional ✿ Modern classic ✿ Classic (old-fashioned)

LIFESTYLE AND HOMESTYLE

Individual dress style and lifestyle/homestyle tend to reflect one another. Look again at the dress style of the person you are buying for. Is he or she neat or messy, modern or traditional?

Think about the things they like to surround themselves with, and make sure that whatever you buy fits in with the general feel. If you try to think outside this box, you'll get it wrong.

Here are some categories of lifestyle that you might recognise. Think about whether these are relevant to you, and feel free to make up some of your own:

Messy (you'll know some of these) ✿ Well organised ✿ Happily cluttered ✿ Obsessively tidy ✿ Colourful ✿ Neutral ✿ Contemporary ✿ Traditional ✿ Retro ✿ Old-fashioned

HOBBIES, SPORTS AND INTERESTS

Present-giving becomes a whole lot simpler if you know the hobbies, sports and general interests of the person you are buying for. It doesn't matter whether it is a family member, friend or colleague; once you've sussed them out, purchasing a gift will always be easy. If he or she loves rugby, tennis, sailing, climbing mountains, going fishing, theatre, opera, art or just collecting fashion (don't we all?), you'll be able to find clever gifts – not just the latest book – that go with their interests; and they'll always be happy and surprised that you're so clever. Tie together the style information (above) with knowledge about how people like to spend their free time and you have all your present answers in an instant.

Here are just a few ideas you'll want to add to:

Sport (which one?) ✿ Cooking, food and drink ✿ Gardening ✿ Photography ✿ Collecting ✿ DIY ✿ Fashion and grooming ✿ Music, films and theatre ✿ Pets ✿ Travel ✿ Cars ✿ Computers and games

LIKES AND DISLIKES

Understanding someone's likes and dislikes can take time. These are usually things that you have to listen out for, and if you're buying for someone you don't know very well, you'll probably never know what constitutes a pet peeve. In this last case, stay safe and keep to the middle of the road. If, however, you recognise a fragrance that they wear, spot a book by a particular author sitting on their desk, or catch them listening to a certain type of music, you're home and dry.

Once you start identifying these areas for each person you're buying for, you'll wonder how you ever chose presents previously, and you'll never want to go back there.

THE GIFT DIARY

Enter all the style notes and discoveries for each person that you buy for in The Gift Diary at the back of this book, and add to them from time to time. That way you'll know exactly what to choose, and it's the best means of keeping all the information together.

ADVANCE NOTICE

It's a good idea to tune in to family and friends throughout the year and listen out for the inevitable hints about what they'd like to buy or be given. You can then jump on the idea when the next gift-giving occasion arises. Those Ugg boots your daughter just admired; that make-up she's hankering after that you think is too expensive for a 17-year-old – those will make perfect presents when her next birthday, or Christmas, comes around (and yes, that's my daughter, and yes, I bought her both – silly me).

In reality there is simply not enough time to do all the research you really need every time you have to buy a gift. But you still want to know that what you're giving is appropriate, conveys the right message, demonstrates your perfect taste and generosity, and contains that all-essential element of surprise. How to achieve all that easily? Store up all those little details and keep them close.

Before I forget – perfect gifts have to be given with perfect timing. Sign up to one of the Special Occasion Reminder Services (see page 223) and input all your important celebration dates. It will only take you a few minutes and will save you rewriting them all into your diary (or remembering to check your birthday book). My book will help you decide what to buy, but it won't ring the alarm when you're about to forget an important date – the reminder service will, though, so you need that too.

Whenever possible, allow yourself enough time to find, order, buy or book whatever it is you choose as a gift. That way you can make full use of the online ordering option, which can make life so much easier – particularly if you have little time to trawl the high street. Trying to find a dozen red roses at your local florist, or book a table at the last minute at that great new restaurant (the one that 'that man – what's his name?' reviewed in *The Sunday Times* a couple of weeks ago), or any table for that matter, unless you're a celebrity) can completely floor you and ruin all your plans. Think ahead – it pays off every time.

1 GIFT OCCASIONS

BIRTHDAYS

I always suggest that you start as early as possible when you're buying presents to give yourself time to think. However, I do say this slightly tongue-in-cheek as I frequently leave it until the last minute – don't we all? If there is a birthday coming up for which you have to buy a present, take a moment to think about the person's outlook/style/interests and stir in the extra 'something' that makes them special. Is he or she a bit bohemian (easy to spot – the beads, the slightly eccentric way of putting clothes together); extra-contemporary (look for raw edges, layers, the latest colours and shapes); modern/classic (look at their shoes and accessories, and the shape of their trousers); or old fashioned (pie-frill shirts and pleated skirts – definitely a problem to but for). Everyone is different. Are you buying for someone who shops at Heals (contemporary, always slightly fashion forward) or in an antique shop (definitely retro or traditional)? Or a mixture of the two?

If you recognise someone's style, it will almost always spill over into their surroundings and everything they do. Tie all of that in with how they like to spend their free time – climbing mountains, playing rugby, going fishing or doing embroidery and you have all your answers in an instant.

In my family I have a Boy Racer/Kitchen Genius, a Sporting Genius, an Adventurer/Gadgetman and a Pampered Princess/Dancing Queen – each with individual style and taste. When I buy gifts for my family I take all that information into account, and I recommend that you do too. For ease of reference, note down the preferences of people you regularly buy for in the Gift Diary at the end of this book.

BIRTHDAY CARDS
(AND CARDS FOR EVERYTHING ELSE AS WELL)

The easiest way to deal with the 'I need a card today but don't have time to buy one' dilemma, is to stock up in advance. Buy a good range, keep them in a special drawer and you'll never be stuck or late again. The following retailers are the perfect place to start:

Charity Cards
www.charitycards.co.uk
This site has lovely cards for every occasion, plus Advent calendars and stocking fillers (for girls). You can also order your printed Christmas cards here, and if you buy ten or more, shipping is free. They'll personalise, gift-wrap and dispatch for you as well.

Clinton Cards
www.clintoncards.co.uk
Here you can buy cards to be sent to you for future use, or order personalised cards that Clinton will send on your behalf. Their reminder service can be used for birthdays and anniversaries. The website is worth a browse as the selection is quite unusual.

Moonpig Cards
www.moonpig.com
This is one of my favourite companies. Moonpig will personalise cards for you and send them out within 24 hours. For Valentine's Day I sent cards from Moonpig at 3 p.m. the previous afternoon and they all arrived in time. How's that for efficiency?

Birthstones

Certain gemstones have become associated with the months of the year, and these are popularly known as birthstones. The stones have varied at different times and in different cultures, but the list given below was established in the UK in 1937 by the National Association of Goldsmiths, and is the one generally used today.

January	Garnet	July	Ruby
February	Amethyst	August	Peridot
March	Aquamarine	September	Sapphire
April	Diamond	October	Opal
May	Emerald	November	Topaz
June	Pearl	December	Turquoise

The Card and Gift Company

www.thecardandgiftcompany.co.uk

Here you'll find cards for all occasions, which they will handwrite on your behalf and send out by first-class post. The address book and reminder service will ensure you never forget that birthday or anniversary again.

Mayther

If you live near any of the places below, pay a visit to one of Mayther's stores, where you'll find a wonderful selection of cards, wrapping paper and gift ideas. They're not online yet, but I hope they will be soon. In the meantime, pop along and take a look.

16 High St, Marlow, Bucks SL7 1AW

1 Old Row Court, Wokingham, Berks RG40 1XZ

35 Bell Street, Henley-on-Thames, Oxon RG9 2BA

15 High Street, Marlborough, Wilts N8 1AA

3 New Inn Hall Street, Oxford OX1 2DH

... AND STAMPS

www.royalmail.com
Go to their 'Buy Online' section to order books of stamps, or your Special Editions or ready-stamped envelopes.

... AND BALLOONS TOO

I think of balloons as being midway between a card and a gift. I've sent balloons (mainly to kids) on lots of occasions and they're always a success. They're more fun than a card, although obviously much more expensive. (Giving balloons is such a tradition in my family that my younger son and daughter are offended when they don't receive one, whereas my oldest son thinks they're a waste of time. Over to you.)

Sky Hi
www.skyhi.co.uk
Sky Hi balloons (motto: 'Inflate someone's day') will deliver anything from a single balloon in a box with your message to a huge bouquet of balloons. They also offer a next-day service, which can be a lifesaver if you've forgotten an important event and want to make a statement.

Amazing Balloons
www.amazingballoons.co.uk
This online balloon store offers a balloon for every occasion you can think of, and they make it extremely easy for you to choose from the huge range. Just click through to the special occasion or type of balloon from the main menu and you're on your way.

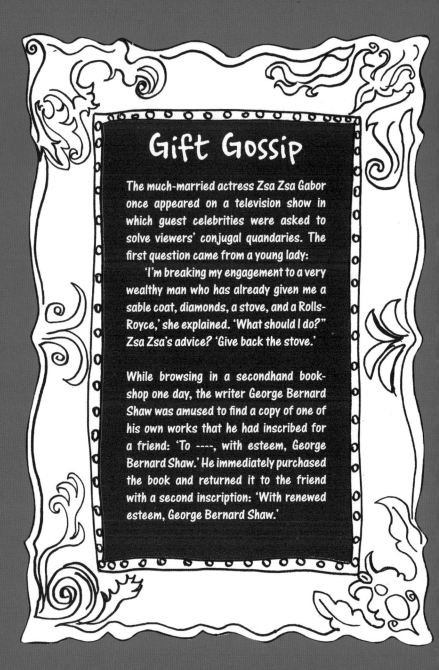

Gift Gossip

The much-married actress Zsa Zsa Gabor once appeared on a television show in which guest celebrities were asked to solve viewers' conjugal quandaries. The first question came from a young lady:

'I'm breaking my engagement to a very wealthy man who has already given me a sable coat, diamonds, a stove, and a Rolls-Royce,' she explained. 'What should I do?"' Zsa Zsa's advice? 'Give back the stove.'

While browsing in a secondhand bookshop one day, the writer George Bernard Shaw was amused to find a copy of one of his own works that he had inscribed for a friend: 'To ----, with esteem, George Bernard Shaw.' He immediately purchased the book and returned it to the friend with a second inscription: 'With renewed esteem, George Bernard Shaw.'

BIRTHDAY CAKES

If, like me, you are not an über-mum who gets out her baking tins the moment a birthday approaches, you'll need to be prepared and order a cake in advance. While there are those among us who are somehow able to make the panto costumes, the fairy cakes and the party surprises while organising everything perfectly – you know the type – most of us find we fall short of perfection and run out of time. Of course you can make the cake if you wish (although my last one had icing that set to a granite-like consistency), but you can also give yourself a break and simply buy a cake from Marks & Spencer or Waitrose. Alternatively, you can visit one of the excellent online bakeries listed on these pages, most of whom have been tried out by yours truly and all of whom are just waiting to create something totally delicious just for you and yours.

Bettys by Post
www.bettysbypost.com
Everything from Bettys by Post is wonderful – I'm a real fan. Whatever you buy, whether it's one of their birthday, Christmas or Simnel cakes, some other teatime goodies or their spectacular Easter eggs, you won't be disappointed. They're gold star winners in my book every time. Some items are shipped worldwide.

Beverly Hills Bakery
www.beverlyhillsbakery.com
The company delivers to North America, Asia and most countries in Europe, but what you can order depends on where you live. Within the UK there's more choice if you live in London than the provinces, but there are large cakes and pretty cupcake gift tins that can be delivered anywhere. A courier service outside London is included in the prices shown.

Cake Toppers

www.caketoppers.co.uk

On this website you can order a birthday cake to be sent for next-day delivery, send your own photo to be used on a cake, or order a birthday or Christmas cake to be sent to anywhere in the mainland UK. Whatever the occasion, you can select a traditional sponge or iced fruit cake to be sent on the date of your choosing. UK delivery; express option.

H P Jung

www.hpjung.com

As this is the place where I order practically all my birthday cakes, I thought they should have a mention. None of my kids will settle for a cake from anywhere else, and I have lost count of how many chocolate or vanilla sponge cakes – iced, beflowered, shaped like rugby balls or balloons – I've bought from here. Orders must be collected from the shops (in Beaconsfield or Gerrards Cross), but the range of cakes can be seen on the website.

Jane Asher

www.jane-asher.co.uk

I'm sure you've heard of Jane Asher: actress, writer and cake designer extraordinaire. If you have the time, you should visit her pretty shop in Chelsea; if not, there's a very good selection of cakes to order online. You will find a choice of about forty different designs for all sorts of different occasions. UK delivery.

Meg Rivers

www.megrivers.com

Meg Rivers has a very tempting website offering 'home-made', beautifully decorated and packaged cakes, biscuits and traybakes (flapjacks, brownies and the like) and I've sampled them many times. For celebration cakes you can choose from rich fruit, chocolate or Victoria sponge. Overseas delivery by request.

Need a Cake
www.need-a-cake.co.uk
There is an amazing selection of cake designs here, including Winnie-the-Pooh and Tigger; guitar- and rugby-ball shaped cakes; and a choice of vanilla Madeira and chocolate fudge cake. This is a family-run cake company that will send most of their cakes anywhere in the UK.

Patisserie Valerie
www.patisserie-valerie.co.uk
The website for this famous patisserie features a mouthwatering array of cakes and desserts that you can order and collect from one of their locations, based mostly in and around London. All the cakes are exquisite both in taste and decoration.

In 2004 Brad Pitt bought Jennifer Aniston a $5 million yacht: the 165ft 'Kalizma', which Richard Burton had given Elizabeth Taylor in 1967, seven years before their first divorce. History repeated itself and Brad and Jen filed for divorce some six months after the gift.

Sara Louise Kakes

**www.saralouisekakes.
co.uk**

Know someone with a sweet
tooth who needs cheering up?
Consider sending a Hansel and
Gretel House cake, decorated
with sugared hearts and flowers; or a box of boozy triple
chocolate and cherry brownies
covered in chocolate fudge icing. Have I got your attention
yet? Thought so. Delivery to
UK mainland only.

*The history of the
birthday cake dates as
far back as the Middle
Ages, when symbolic
items, such as gold coins,
rings and thimbles,
each associated with a
particular prediction,
would be hidden
inside cakes*

The Cake Store

www.thecakestore.com

The Cake Store offers hand-crafted cakes in a superb range of
designs for all types of occasion, from birthdays to weddings; but
bear in mind that they deliver only within the M25 unless by special arrangement. Prices include delivery, and you need to allow
7–10 days for your order to arrive.

The English Cheese-cake Company

www.cheesecake.co.uk

There's everything here for
cheesecake addicts, from Chocolate Toffee Walnut Smash and
Raspberry Split to Charlie's
Original New York New York

*Not everyone marks
birthdays: the Poles,
for example, have
name day celebra-
tions instead.*

Double-baked cheesecake, and many more too numerous to list.
You can order yours personalised for birthdays and other celebrations. UK delivery; express option.

VALENTINE'S DAY

*E*very year on Valentine's Day, hundreds of thousands of roses wing their way across countries around the world. Your local postman is weighed down under the volume of all those cards and packages, restaurants gear up for the onslaught, and girls and boys everywhere wait in trepidation to find out whether or not the postman is going to knock at their door. Oh, the worry! The thought of having to pretend you received a card when maybe you didn't, the shiver of excitement when you think that today is possibly the day he'll propose (and let's not think about afterwards if he doesn't), and the huge, huge problem of what to wear when you go out to that romantic restaurant for dinner. Yes, Valentine's Day is truly a serious occasion.

The key to making the day a success is to take action well in advance. Wait till the last minute and those roses will be sold out, all the tables at your favourite restaurant will be booked, and your card could well be late. Get planning right away. Here's my list of the gifts you might like to consider and where to find them: ideas for unusual and special gifts from flowers to diamonds, and finally, if you're in the mood to splash out, some exceptional places to shop.

> *'Love is a smoke*
> *made with the*
> *fume of sighs.'*
> WILLIAM SHAKESPEARE

FLOWERS

You don't have to give roses, although these are the traditional flowers of Valentine's Day. But believe me, a bunch of flowers hastily grabbed at your local garage will not do, at least not if you want the relationship to last. If you want to make a deep and enduring impression, walking through the door with a beautifully hand-tied bunch of the deepest red flowers will work every time.

If possible, preferably at least a week in advance, visit the following websites, where you can order roses in inspired alternative arrangements, plus, in many cases, champagne and chocolates.

Imogen Stone
www.imogenstone.co.uk
This is one of my favourite places for flowers and it's totally unsurprising that their order book is usually full as Valentine's Day approaches. They're not just an online florist, but a luxury gift store as well. Once you've chosen your bouquet, you can include Rococo chocolate truffles, Abahna toiletries, scented candles and LSA vases as well. Nationwide and same-day delivery.

Jane Packer
www.janepackerdelivered.com
Jane Packer is one of the most famous floral designers, and having sent her flowers several times, I know that anything you buy here will be totally beautiful and special. The arrangements are carefully thought-out pieces of art, such as glossy tulips in a dramatic scarlet vase, or a pink hat box filled with roses in shades of pink. Everything is in her unique, chic style. Nationwide delivery online.

Jane Wadham Flowers
www.jwflowers.com
Jane Wadham is a UK florist widely regarded as one of London's leading floral designers. The website is lovely and clear, and offers

a small collection of beautiful and unique ideas for Valentine's Day and other occasions. Expect to spend a bit more here but whatever you choose will be so beautifully presented that it's well worth it. UK delivery; express option.

Moyses Flowers
www.moysesflowers.co.uk

You won't save money at this long-established florist (founded 1876), and this isn't the place for your standard bunch of red roses, but you will find some original suggestions for Valentine's Day that you won't find anywhere else. They also offer bubbles, baskets and couture chocolates. Delivery nationwide.

Rossi & Rovetti Flowers
www.rossirovetti.com

Rossi & Rovetti is a quite exceptional flower store based in San Francisco. Everything here is lovely and different, and alongside the Valentine and congratulations suggestions there's the 'Cocktail' collection, where the arrangements have names such as Mojhito and Green Apple Martini, and 'English Florals'. Same-day delivery available to most worldwide destinations.

Serenata Flowers
www.serenataflowers.com

This is an online florist with a very clear website where you'll discover an extremely good selection of flowers in various price ranges. The selection menus are easy to use and you can choose your flower style from contemporary, elegant or simple. Select the type of bouquet, the price you want to pay or the variety of flower. There's a wide selection for international delivery.

For more online florists, all of whom offer special occasion selections, take a look at the main Flowers section (page 194).

DID YOU KNOW THAT ...

♥ The history of Valentine's Day, and even of St Valentine himself, isn't totally clear. We know that the day contains elements of both Christian and ancient Roman tradition, and we also know that at least three different saints named Valentine are recognised by the Catholic Church as having been martyred.

♥ One story goes that Valentine was a priest who lived during the third century AD in Rome and defied Emperor Claudius II by marrying young lovers after the practice had been outlawed. Others suggest that he might have been killed for trying to help Christians escape the harsh Roman prisons.

♥ According to one legend, Valentine sent the first Valentine's card whilst in prison, to a young girl who visited him and who may or may not have been the daughter of his prison guard.

♥ Pope Gelasius declared 14 February St Valentine's Day around AD 498, and the oldest known Valentine greeting still in existence today is a poem written by Charles, Duke of Orleans to his wife while he was imprisoned in the Tower of London following his capture at the Battle of Agincourt. The greeting, which was written in 1415, is part of the manuscript collection at the British Library.

♥ The first written record of the association between Valentine's Day and romantic love is in 'Parlement of Foules' (1382) by Geoffrey Chaucer, which was written in honour of the first anniversary of the engagement of King Richard II of England to Anne of Bohemia. They were married around the age of 14.

♥ Oh yes, and roughly 35 per cent of all diamonds purchased throughout the year are bought on Valentine's Day. Keep your hopes up, girls!

SAY IT WITH CHOCOLATES?

Boys, be aware that chocolates are not really the best gift to give on Valentine's Day, as they beg the question, 'Why wasn't I good enough for roses?' However, if you're accompanying them with a single rose and a bottle of bubbles, and you know that your love has a penchant for soft centres, they *can* go down a treat. Most chocolate boutiques offer special selections for Valentine's Day, as well as for every other occasion you can think of. Here are a few that make a really special effort, with a wide range of prices, lovely packaging and in many cases the option to include that bottle of fizz as well. The roses you'll have to buy elsewhere.

Amelie Chocolate
www.ameliechocolat.co.uk
Heart-shaped boxes (with heart-shaped chocolates inside), miniature gift boxes and champagne truffles are just some of the continental chocolates you can order here, with a unique selection of freshly made delicacies from Belgium, Holland, France and Germany. Ships worldwide; express UK delivery.

Brownes Chocolates
www.brownes.co.uk
Award-winning Brownes offers luxurious hand-made chocolates in four sizes of box (including some that are heart-shaped) ranging from 60g to their 1kg presentation box. There are also after-dinner 'mint chasers', buttered brazils, party crackers, dusted almonds and chocolate covered raisins. Worldwide delivery.

Chouchoute Chocolatier
www.chouchoute.co.uk
This Birmingham-based chocolatier, created by Pierre Soualah, former *traiteur* at the upmarket Fauchon in Paris, offers fabulous pampering chocolates from gift boxes to hampers, and although

the range is quite small, I'm sure, like me, you'll find it extremely hard to resist. Express UK delivery.

Hotel Chocolat

www.hotelchocolat.co.uk

Send someone a Chocogram Deluxe or champagne truffles, or choose from Hotel Chocolat's special occasion selections. For Valentine's Day there are fun ideas, such as the 'Dipping Adventure for Two', 'The Chocolatier's Table' or 'Liquid Chocolate Kiss Mix'. Ships worldwide; express UK delivery.

Melt Chocolates

www.meltchocolates.com

Order one of Melt's signature chocolate hearts and hide your special message inside. Alternatively, choose raspberry and white chocolate bonbons, sea-salted caramels, champagne truffles or a box of seventy hand-picked delights. UK delivery; express option.

JEWELS

If that 5-carat diamond engagement ring is on your shopping list this Valentine's Day, you probably know already where you're going to buy it from. All I will say is do be careful; you need to be sure you are buying from a reputable source so that you get the best quality and the best price. There are loads of people offering 'diamonds for less', but you simply won't get the best clarity, cut, colour or carat (see, I know my four Cs) if you try to do this cheaply. You want a good deal but you also want a really high-quality stone. I suggest you shop around. Yes, talk to Tiffany, talk to Garrard, and talk to your local jeweller. Learn as much as you can. Don't pay a fortune for the name, but do buy the best you can afford – after all, you're only going to be doing this once, aren't you?

Mark Walker, diamond expert extraordinaire for www.icecool. co.uk, advises not to be blinded by science and mystery when buying a diamond. He offers the following advice:

BUYING DIAMONDS: THE GOLDEN RULES

1 *Spend as much as you can afford. You will get a better quality, more smiles from the recipient and your investment will be more fruitful.*

2 *Choose the best clarity range – VS2 and better. Your diamond will be purer.*

3 *Choose the best colour range – D to G. Your diamond will be whiter and brighter.*

4 *Choose only fine-quality cut, proportions and finish. Your diamond will be more radiant.*

5 *In terms of caratage, size is certainly not everything, but large diamonds of 3 carats plus have increased in value by approximately 40 per cent over the past two years.*

6 *Shape is very much a personal choice, but in terms of popularity, 60 per cent of diamons are round, 15 per cent are princess, 15 per cent are emerald, and 10 per cent are fancy shapes, such as pear.*

7 *Always make sure that your diamond has an official laboratory certificate. This verifies the characteristics and size of the diamond by a third party, and is likely to be issued by GIA, HRD or IGI.*

8 *Take advice from a diamond expert or jeweller who understands diamonds and can take you through all the sparkling options, particularly if you're considering a stone 5 carats or above.'*

On to other Valentine jewels... Whatever you decide to spend, you want the whole effect to be totally gorgeous. Here are a few of my favourite jewellery stores, all with an online presence, and most with galleries and showrooms where you can browse if you have the time. Also take a look at the Jewel Collector section (page 152) for other ideas.

Astley Clarke
www.astleyclarke.com

Clever, luxury online jewellery boutique Astley Clarke carries exquisite contemporary, fine and designer jewellery collections from all over the world, and is the perfect place to find romantic jewellery gifts. The website is beautifully designed and it's extremely easy to find something pretty. They also offer luxury packaging, next-day delivery in the UK and express delivery worldwide.

Dinny Hall
www.dinnyhall.com

Here you can see beautifully designed, well-priced modern jewellery from one of Britain's foremost jewellery designers. Every piece is hand-crafted using high-quality silver or gold and a variety of precious or semi-precious stones. If you haven't discovered Dinny Hall's work until now, this is definitely the time to start collecting. Worldwide delivery and gift wrapping available.

Emma Chapman Jewels
www.emmachapmanjewels.com

Emma Chapman is a London Fashion Week jewellery designer, who creates beautiful, exotic and opulent gemstone jewellery inspired by ancient eras, such as Baroque, Mughal and Elizabethan, but gives it a modern twist. The jewels are grouped by names such as Beach Babe, Baroque Goddess and Indian Princess. Everything is reasonably priced. Call for next-day delivery.

Howarth Gallery

www.howarth-gallery.co.uk

George Jensen, Baccarat and Shaune Leane are some of the contemporary jewellery designers you'll find amongst this gallery's truly marvellous collection. This is the perfect place to find something really special, offering a range you're unlikely to find all together in the shops. Worldwide delivery.

WISPS OF LACE

Needless to say, you have to know your Valentine pretty well to buy them something minute, slinky and sexy, and you must of course get the size absolutely right. Too small or too large and you could land yourself in big trouble either way (think about it). Lingerie is, of course, an extremely popular gift, and there are lots of places to buy from both on and offline. You might think that you won't get a great deal of help if you order online, but these retailers specialise in offering advice on what to buy. Use their online guides or call them up, taking care to filch something first from her lingerie drawer (without getting caught) to help you with the size. I'm not sure what excuse you can use if you get caught with one of her bras in your coat pocket: I'll leave that one up to you!

'If love is blind, why is lingerie so popular?'

ANON

Agent Provocateur

www.agentprovocateur.com

Don't shop here if you're looking for something in a size larger than a 36E or if you want a website without atmosphere. Do come here if you love their products and don't want to have to go the store to find them. Ships worldwide; express option plus gorgeous packaging.

Glamorous Amorous

www.glamorousamorous.com

This glamorous online boutique specialises in lingerie you won't easily find anywhere else – think animal print and scarlet trim from Fifi Chachnil, sequin and silk camisoles from Guia La Bruna and a lace bustier and thong from Bacirubati. UK mainland delivery is free, and they'll deliver speedily worldwide too.

La Senza

www.lasenza.co.uk

La Senza is known for offering a clever and well-priced range of lingerie and has shops all over the UK, plus an excellent website. The online service is excellent and you'll always find something special, from red satin and black lace lingerie to basques, bustiers and suspenders. Ships worldwide; express option and gift wrapping available.

Myla

www.myla.com

Here you'll find seriously beautiful satin and lace lingerie in colours such as brown plum, peach and Yves blue, black and ivory. Then there are tulle thongs and hipsters, plus a sensual range of candles and accessories. Ships worldwide; express option and gift wrapping available.

Silk Storm

www.silkstorm.com

This is an online-only lingerie boutique offering luxury French and Italian brands, with collections including Aubade, Valery, Argentovivo, Cotton Club and Barbara. Everything is beautifully photographed and the sizing help is excellent, although don't expect anything to go much above a 36D. Ships worldwide; express option and gift wrapping available.

NEVER DO THESE

✗ Never buy a bunch of flowers from a garage – they are almost always nasty and will make it even more obvious that you forgot.

✗ Never buy paste jewellery on Valentine's Day. If you can't afford diamonds, there are wonderful jewels set with semi-precious stones. You don't have to go for hearts, but buy something pretty in a colour you know she wears.

✗ Never buy jewellery at all unless you're prepared to spend the time choosing something you know she'll like.

✗ Never buy lingerie in the wrong size. Never guess. I've said it before, but I really mean it. Trouble awaits you there.

✗ Never buy chocolates if you know she's on a diet. It's just mean and you'll probably end up eating them yourself.

✗ Never forget the card and the flowers; and don't forget to book a table in your favourite restaurant well in advance – you almost certainly will not get in at the last moment. (On that point I'd just like to thank Rose at San Lorenzo for helping me out when my tardy son decided he wanted to take his girlfriend somewhere special last Valentine's Day. You're a star and I'm very grateful. I promise he'll think ahead, next time.)

AND FINALLY …

It really is the thought that counts. You don't have to spend more than you can afford on a huge bunch of roses, and you don't have to buy the jewels, the chocs, the lacy lingerie and the expensive meal. One single beautiful red rose says exactly the same thing: 'I'm thinking about you'. That's what matters, after all.

MOTHER'S DAY

Without any doubt the most important thing about Mother's Day is for kids to show that they care. It doesn't matter how big or small the gift is, or if there is one at all, it's definitely the thought that counts, and wherever you are and whatever you're doing you need to call or send a card.

In my household there's usually a frantic rush either early on the morning of Mother's Day or the day before to go out and buy cards and flowers. I have, on many occasions, been brought breakfast in bed (well, up until the time when my kids forgot that there was such a thing as morning).

The traditional gifts for Mother's Day are flowers and cakes, although fragrance, chocolates and champagne always work well too, alongside anything created at home, such as a photo frame with a recent photo, or home-made cards and pictures. Here are my ideas on where and what to buy for Mother's Day. You can also take a look at the flower shops in Valentine's Day and in the main Flowers section (see pages 30 and 194).

> *'All women become like their mothers. That is their tragedy. No man does. That's his.'*
>
> OSCAR WILDE, *THE IMPORTANCE OF BEING EARNEST*

FLOWERS

Giving flowers is one of the best ways to show that you haven't forgotten Mother's Day, as wherever you are in the world you can organise flowers to be sent. Notice that I said 'wherever you are', because with the internet and the mobile phone there's absolutely no excuse. You don't have to spend a fortune; in fact 'over the top' doesn't really work on Mother's Day. Beautiful and on time are the watchwords here, so don't forget. When choosing which flowers to give, pay some attention to what you know she likes – is your mother a lily person or a rose lover? Does she like modern flowers or traditional arrangements? Make next Mother's Day even more special with just a little extra thought. *See also page 194.*

David Austin Roses

www.davidaustinroses.com

David Austin is famous for developing new types of English roses; his first, 'Constance Spry', was launched in 1963. On his website you can find many varieties, including modern hybrid tea roses and floribundas, climbing roses, ramblers, modern shrub roses and wild species. These can be supplied in containers or hand-tied bouquets, and can be delivered throughout Europe.

Forever Flowering

www.foreverflowering. co.uk

Forever Flowering is based near Kew Gardens in London and has a mission to create elegant arrangements that are not

'The hand that rocks the cradle usually is attached to someone who isn't getting enough sleep.'

JOHN FIEBIG

over- designed but have the feel of freshly picked flowers. They offer a gorgeous range of hand-tied bunches, the prettiest flower baskets, glorious rose bouquets and scented flowers. Next-day delivery is available throughout the UK.

Hayes Florist
www.hayesflorist.co.uk

The designs here are essentially modern and beautifully photographed so that you can see exactly what you're ordering, from the hand-tied Heavenly Rose to the Mother's Day Blissful Basket and Tulip Splash. You can include chocolates, balloons, champagne and candles with your order. Ships worldwide; same-day delivery in UK.

Paula Pryke Flowers
www.paula-pryke-flowers.com

Paula Pryke is known as one of the most innovative florists in the world. You can visit one of her shops or choose from her designs online and then call or email to order. Bouquets without vases can be sent throughout the UK, while those with vases can be sent to addresses with London postcodes.

The Real Flower Company
www.realflowers.co.uk

The Real Flower Company is different from many online florists in that they're dedicated to the small-scale production of roses, garden foliage and scented herbs that are chosen for their looks, texture and scent. Everything is beautifully presented, making this a perfect source of gifts for lots of different occasions. UK delivery; express option.

Roses and Blooms
www.rosesandblooms.com

Roses and Blooms are based in Lexington Avenue, New York. They will deliver most of their flower designs wherever you are in the world, so whether on holiday or living abroad, you have no excuse not to send flowers on Mother's Day. Their lovely designs are different from those you will find elsewhere.

CLEVER CAKES AND OTHER FOODIE TREATS

Make a card, bake some cakes or arrange simple but pretty flowers on Mother's Day and you'll definitely be winning. I have kids who don't make cards or bake (except for my older son in Scotland) or arrange flowers, so I'll be happy with that beautiful bouquet, box of fairy cakes, Chanel bath bubbles or bottle of Wild Goose. I'm not fussy, as I'm sure you can tell – just don't forget or you'll be in real trouble. Be a bit careful here that you choose something you know she loves – chocs to a mum who's just gone on a diet will not make you flavour of the month, however gorgeous they are.

Biscuiteers

www.biscuiteers.com

Give something fun and different the next time you want to say 'Happy Mother's Day' (or anything else for that matter) and send a gorgeous tin of wonderfully iced biscuits from Biscuiteers. There's the Bootilicious Shoes tin, the Oodles of Poodles tin and the Creepy Crawlies tin. UK delivery.

Clearwater Hampers

www.hamper.com

From the 'Mums Breakfast in Bed' hamper to the fuchsia-coloured hatbox of high-quality truffles and freshly cut daffodils there are plenty of reasonably priced ideas here for Mother's Day (and all the other gift-giving occasions). Worldwide delivery.

Coco à Moi

www.cocoamoi.com

This is chocolate brownie heaven, where you can buy a three-tier cakestand piled high with brownies, or hand-finished boxes of bite-sized brownies for wedding favours, and party gifts and beautifully wrapped gift boxes containing flavours such as dark chocolate and orange, chocolate and mint, and chocolate and pecan. Ships worldwide; express UK delivery and gift wrap.

For Goodness Cake

www.forgoodnesscake.co.uk

The daintiest fairy cakes, prettily packaged in a high-quality, pale blue box tied with fuchsia ribbon, are on offer here. They're freshly baked, so they need to be eaten quickly and you can order champagne, a strawberry plant, or Whittard's Columbian coffee to go with them. UK delivery within 48 hours.

Fortnum & Mason

www.fortnumandmason.co.uk

As you would expect, Fortnum & Mason offer a wonderful range of ideas for all occasions, from Mother's Day to Christmas. There are sweets and chocolates galore, beautifully packaged teas and coffees, and pretty pampering ideas as well. Worldwide delivery.

The Original Hat Box Cake Company

www.theoriginalhatboxcakecompany.co.uk

Pretty and original ideas include the exquisite Mother's Day Cake and Gold Cup Cake Hat Box, the whimsical Pink Handbag (no, not a real one) and Teapot Hat Boxes. Other celebration cakes and beautifully iced Christmas cakes are on offer too. Delivers nationwide; express option.

Thorntons

www.thorntons.co.uk

Thorntons are always extremely clever at offering special gift ideas to tie in with whatever 'gifty' occasion is in the offing. For Mother's Day there are chocolate gift suggestions, plus hampers and flowers (mine's the Amazing Mum Bouquet) and everything is reasonably priced and beautifully packaged. Ships most products worldwide; express UK delivery.

FRAGRANT SUGGESTIONS

I love to be given gorgeously scented candles on Mother's Day. Unlike perfume, it's not necessary to get the fragrance absolutely right. Just pick one that your mother knows and likes; don't try to think too far 'outside the box'. If she loves the scent of roses, most high-quality products in that fragrance will please her; but if you've never known her to choose rose-scented products, don't go there. She already knows what she likes.

Amara

www.amara.co.uk

This is a really lovely online home accessories and gift website with some unusual products that aren't always the easiest to find, including Gianna Rose Atelier soaps, Millefiori, Baobag and Claus Porto candles, and Lothantique and Welton Design fragrance diffusers. Worldwide and express delivery plus gift wrapping.

Ancienne Ambiance

www.ancienneambiance.com

Everything here is unique and really fragrant with luxurious packaging, so if you're in a hurry, you just need to choose a card to go with one of the products and you're away. The Cornucopia bathsalts, Goddess Body Box and Rose and Jasmine candles will give you inspiration. All prices include worldwide delivery and free gift wrapping.

Content Beauty

www.beingcontent.com

Content Beauty sources natural fragrance and beauty products from around the world. Here you can shop here in a friendly boutique environment for luxurious and unusual pampering brands, such as Suzanne aux Bains and Tsi-La. Ships worldwide; express UK delivery.

Cologne & Cotton

www.cologneandcotton.com

This is a very special shop and website offering some unusual and hard to find bath and body products and fragrances by Diptyque, Cath Collins, La Compagnie de Provence, Côté Bastide, Annik Goutal, Coudray and Rosine. Ships worldwide; express UK delivery and gift wrapping.

Jo Malone

www.jomalone.co.uk

Jo Malone has become the easiest destination for luxurious and fragrant gifts for all occasions. The fragrances are gorgeous, the gifts are wonderful, the packaging superb and yes, I've bought there many times. Choose from White Jasmine and Mint Body Crème, Red Rose Cologne or one of the scented candles. Whatever you select, you won't go wrong here. Express UK delivery and gift packaging.

Laline

www.laline.co.uk

Laline is relatively new range of bath, bodycare and home accessories, hand-made with natural oils and fragrances, all sourced in France and beautifully packaged. The range includes soaps, body creams, body oils and face masks, plus products for men, babies and home. UK delivery; express option.

Woodruffs of Winchester

www.woodruffs.co.uk

This fragrance and gift retailer offers a very good range of bath, body and fragrance products by Roger et Gallet, Diptyque, Cath Collins, Kenneth Turner, Crabtree & Evelyn, Floris and Jane Packer. They'll deliver anywhere in the world, offer an express delivery service for the UK, and are happy to gift wrap for you.

DID YOU KNOW THAT ...

❀ *There are various theories about the origin of Mother's Day. Some claim that it comes from the custom of mother worship in ancient Greece, being related to the festival of Cybele, a renowned mother of Greek gods.*

❀ *Matronalia was another day devoted to mothers that ancient Romans celebrated. It was actually dedicated to Juno, queen of the gods, although mothers were usually given gifts on that day.*

❀ *In the UK Mother's Day falls on the fourth Sunday of Lent (or three weeks before Easter Sunday). It is thought to originate from the 16th-century Christian practice of servants and apprentices being released by their masters to visit their families – possibly the only day of the year when such a reunion was possible.*

❀ *Those returning home often took a fruit cake with them, known as a Simnel cake, which is now usually consumed at Easter.*

❀ *In the USA Mother's Day is celebrated on the second Sunday in May. Although inspired by the British Mothering Sunday, it was imported by the social activist Julia Ward Howe after the American Civil War and intended as a call to unite women against war. In 1870 Julia Ward wrote the Mother's Day Proclamation as a call for peace and disarmament. The day wasn't formally recognised until 1907, and was first celebrated in Grafton, West Virginia, on 10 May 1908. It was declared an official national holiday in 1914 by President Woodrow Wilson – a day for US citizens to show the flag in honour of those mothers who had lost sons to war.*

❀ *According to the National Restaurant Association, Mother's Day is now the most popular day of the year to dine out at a restaurant in the USA.*

SPAS AND SALONS

My family knows that I love to be given a beautifully packaged gift voucher for my local spa – Mulberries in Beaconsfield. It beats any salon I've been to anywhere. If you know your mother's favourite spa or salon, do consider gift vouchers. My advice is not to choose which treatment to give – you'll be sure to choose a manicure at the very moment she's desperate for a back massage. Pay your money, get your voucher, wrap it beautifully (if they don't do it for you) and you're done.

If you're in doubt about which spa to choose, simply look at the websites below and select from their lists.

Spa Break
www.spabreak.co.uk

Spa Break offers comprehensive information on luxury spas all over the country, with plenty of information and pictures to help you to choose. You can purchase a gift voucher for a specific monetary value, or for a specific type of break.

SpaFinder
www.spafinder.com

This is much more than just a global spa locator. Here you can easily find out about spas anywhere in the world and also see the specific services they offer. You can also contact them directly through the website's links. There are so many wonderful pictures of each spa that, if you're anything like me, you'll want to book something immediately.

'A mother is a person who, seeing there are only four pieces of pie for five people, promptly announces she never did care for pie.'

TENNEVA JORDAN

EASTER

*E*aster is the oldest Christian holiday and the most important day of the church year. It celebrates the resurrection of Christ three days after his death by crucifixion.

The origin of the word 'Easter' is not certain, but it most probably comes from Estre, or Eostre, the name of an Anglo-Saxon goddess of spring. The German word *Ostern* has the same derivation, but most other languages follow the Greek term that was used by early Christians: *pascha*, from the Hebrew *pesach*, or Passover.

> *'All I really need is love, but a little chocolate now and then doesn't hurt!'*
> LUCY VAN PELT IN 'PEANUTS' (CHARLES SCHULTZ)

EASTER TRADITIONS

SIMNEL CAKE

For many Christians, the forty-day period of fasting and repentance in preparation for Easter, otherwise known as Lent, ends in a feast of seasonal and symbolic foods. In the late 17th century, on the fourth Sunday of Lent, girls working in service would take home to their mothers a rich fruit cake enriched with marzipan, known as Simnel cake. This might have been the only day of the year that the whole family got together. The cake was decorated with eleven marzipan balls representing the apostles – the twelfth one (Judas) omitted because he betrayed Christ.

WHERE TO BUY EASTER CAKES

Bettys by Post

www.bettysbypost.co.uk

I'm totally addicted to this website, which offers wonderful cakes and cookies linked to the time of year. At Easter you'll find Simnel cake, miniature eggs, chick and rabbit biscuits, chocolate lambs and bunnies, and a totally original range of Easter eggs, from the reasonably priced and prettily decorated high-quality chocolate kind right up to Betty's Imperial Easter Egg containing 5kg of chocolate. Well, I ask you, who would settle for anything less?

Dukeshill

www.dukeshillham.co.uk

Apart from its wonderful meat products (see page 107), Dukeshill also makes great cakes. Next-day delivery to most of UK.

Fortnum & Mason

www.fortnumandmason.com

See page 45.

Meg Rivers

www.megrivers.com

See page 25.

The Simply Delicious Fruit Cake Company

www.simplydeliciouscakes.co.uk

Simply Delicious Cakes is an online cake bakery with a small but well-photographed range of fruitcake-based products, including Highland fruitcakes, Christmas cakes, the 'Shropshire Game-keeper', with mixed spice and sloe gin, the New Discovery, with apricots, stem ginger and brandy, and a luscious-looking Simnel cake. In all cases you can buy their cakes with or without a tin to give them away in.

Hot Cross Buns

+ The Greeks and Egyptians ate small cakes or buns in honour of the respective goddesses that they worshipped, and buns marked with a cross were eaten by the Saxons to honour their goddess Eostre. Hot cross buns are traditionally eaten on Good Friday, with the cross standing as a symbol of the crucifixion.

+ In Australia a chocolate version of the bun has become popular, with cocoa and chocolate chips being added to the dough.

+ In the Czech Republic 'mazanec' is similar bun and often has a cross on top.

+ In the Maldives 'jehi banas' (cream buns) are a particular favourite of the locals at Easter time.

EASTER EGGS

Eggs have been associated with Easter celebrations throughout history. In ancient times the egg was a symbol of fertility and new beginnings. Christians adopted this symbol to represent the resurrection.

In the UK and Europe the first Easter Eggs weren't made of chocolate; they were painted and decorated duck, goose or hen eggs. This tradition remains in some parts of the world today. With the passage of time, the decoration has become more and more elaborate, with images of flowers and animals, colourful patterns, and gold and silver leaf details being incorporated.

The first chocolate Easter eggs appeared in Germany and France in the early 19th century, and their popularity spread quickly to the rest of Europe and beyond. The first eggs were solid chocolate, but these were followed by hollow eggs, which were much harder to make at that time. Eventually, the development of modern chocolate-making processes helped the chocolate egg to become the Easter gift of choice worldwide.

THE FABERGÉ STORY

The most famous Easter eggs of all must be the enamelled and jewel-encrusted gold eggs that French jeweller Carl Fabergé was commissioned to make for the Russian imperial family. The first was made in 1885 as a gift from Tsar Alexander III to the empress Maria Fedorovna. Over the years a total of fifty-four eggs were made, all of them exquisite objects of unique design, and each containing a surprise. The collection was dispersed around the world after the Russian Revolution and only forty-two of these fabulous eggs survive.

A Fabergé egg created in 1902 for the Rothschild banking family was sold in London in 2007 for £8.9 million.

WHERE TO BUY EASTER EGGS

If you think ahead, you can choose from the most wonderful selection of Easter eggs, including from:

Bettys by Post

www.bettysbypost.co.uk
See page 52.

The Chocolate Trading Company

www.chocolatetradingco.com

Here you will find a mouth-watering selection of chocolates from Charbonel et Walker's serious chocolate indulgences and chocoholics' hampers to funky and fun ideas such as chocolate sardines and Jungle Crunch. There are lots of suggestions for Easter in various price ranges. UK delivery; express option and gift wrapping.

Fortnum & Mason

www.fortnumandmason.com
See page 45.

Hotel Chocolat

www.hotelchocolat.co.uk
See page 34.

Also see Chocolates, page 192.

DID YOU KNOW THAT ...

✦ *In Latin, 'Easter' is* Festa Paschalia; *in French,* Paques; *in Italian,* Pasqua; *in Dutch,* Paschen; *in Spanish,* Pascua; *in Danish,* Paaske; *and in-Swedish,* Pask.

✦ *Easter is a movable feast, and the date it falls on is governed by a calculation relating to the spring equinox. The actual formula (much simplified) is that the first Sunday after the first full moon following the spring equinox is Easter Sunday. This formula was set by Egyptian astronomers in Alexandra in AD 235 and calculated using the same method as the Jews have traditionally used to calculate the feast of Passover, which occurred at about the same time as the crucifixion.*

FATHER'S DAY

I always think that it's harder to get it right on Father's day than on many other occasions, well it certainly is in our house. A card is essential but you also have to put your thinking cap on to find something that doesn't look too easy, nor contrived. Doing this kind of shopping on the web does make matters so much easier. Yes, you have to allow extra time, but think how long it might otherwise take you to find that personalised champagne bottle label, rare bottle of whisky or signed copy of a book by his favourite author.

If he falls into one of the recipient categories below, such as Boy Racer, Adventurer or Sporting Genius then you'll probably find the solution there; alternatively, for books both old and new, take a look in Bookworm; and for booze look in the Wine and Champagne section. Otherwise browse the following pages for plenty more options at a wide range of prices.

GADGETS AND GAMES

Only buy gadgets or games on Father's Day if you know that he likes that kind of thing and will use them. A gift is not just a 'gift' no matter how beautifully wrapped, and it's essential to put the necessary thought into what you're doing. If he plays chess – fine, get him a chess set; but if you've never seen him set out a board then forget it, he's almost certainly not going to start learning now.

Chess Baron

www.chessbaron.co.uk

If your dad *is* a chess enthusiast you'll almost certainly find something for him here. This retailer based in Taunton, Somerset, offers over 100 artisan-made chess boards and pieces. Worldwide delivery.

The first Father's Day church service in the USA was held on 5 July 1908 in Fairmont, West Virginia, inspired by a mine explosion that killed 361 men, many of them fathers.

Farscape Games

www.farscapegames.co.uk

Whatever game you play as a family, that you know he enjoys, you'll find it here – whether it's Mah Jong, Monopoly, dominoes, backgammon or bridge – alongside poker, roulette, Scrabble and Diplomacy. It's extremely easy to buy from this website and they offer speedy worldwide delivery.

Micro Anvica

www.microanvica.com

Computing, photography, audio, iPod, SatNav, TV and radio are the main areas here, with brands such as iPod, Belkin, Epson, Logitech, Sony and Tom Tom being just a few. The shops and the website are more user-friendly than many, so if you have a really useful gadget-loving dad this would a great place to shop. Ships worldwide; express UK delivery.

Oregon Scientific

www.oregonscientific.co.uk

Oregon Scientific, established in the US in 1989, creates electronic products for modern lifestyles. As well as their stylish wireless weather stations and thermometers they supply the world's slimmest radio controlled alarm clock plus loads more ideas. UK delivery; express option.

Paramount Zone

www.paramountzone.com

Paramount Zone offers an extensive and carefully selected choice of gadgets, games, boy's toys, bar items, sports gadgets, mp3 players, executive items/toys, bachelor pad stuff, gift ideas, and lifestyle accessories – and these are just some of the items you'll find. Worldwide and express UK delivery.

> *As far as gadgets are concerned, they have to be functional. Hear that word? It's essential. Anything non-functional is a waste of money, space and time.*

The Gadget Shop

www.thegadgetshop.com

Browse the online catalogue for some of the funniest, coolest gadgets you can buy. They have everything from the frivolous to the functional, the digital to the down right silly. You'll find big boy's toys, retro toys, fun stuff, Star Wars and ipod accessories here too. Ships worldwide; express UK delivery and gift wrapping.

The Sharp Edge

www.thesharperedge.co.uk

Originally in the mobile phone industry, this retailer branched into up-to-the-minute gadgets and gifts about five years ago, and aims to keep you informed about the latest ideas on the market. It's a really excellent store offering you clever and unusual suggestions plus innovative accessories. Ships worldwide; express UK delivery and gift wrapping.

For more ideas, see also Gadget Crazy, page 142.

President Calvin Coolidge recommended that Father's Day became a national holiday in 1924.

EXPERIENCE AND ACTIVITY DAYS

I always seem to repeat myself when I'm talking about this type of gift, so my apologies, but I'm going to do it again. Firstly, do make sure that your dad already enjoys the sort of day out or adventure that you're planning for him, and then make sure that whatever you buy is going to be used within the time allowed. There's a huge range of 'experiences' on offer, and you can spend a very reasonable amount, or you can spend 'the earth', but whatever your choice, it can be extremely frustrating to know that that voucher is languishing in a drawer and hasn't been used. Take control here, really, and make sure that it happens. Yes I am talking from experience, twice.

Great Experience Days
www.greatexperiencedays.co.uk
There are some really good Father's Day gift ideas here. Choose from (among loads of other ideas) an off-road driving day, driving a Ferrari or Porsche 996, dual control flying lessons or clay pigeon shooting. Worldwide voucher delivery; express service in UK.

'When I was a boy of fourteen, my father was so ignorant I could hardly stand to have the old man around. But when I got to be twenty-one, I was astonished at how much the old man had learned in seven years.'

MARK TWAIN

Red Letter Days
www.redletterdays.co.uk
One of the best 'Experience' day providers, Red Letter Days makes it easy for you to choose between flying, driving and some serious adventure experiences. They also offer great rally day options, plus luxuries, such as lunch on the Orient Express. Once you've ordered, it will be sent out in an attractive gift pack to the recipient.

SMOKES AND ACCESSORY GIFTS

Whether you approve or not, if your dad is a dyed-in-the-wool cigar smoker, you are not going to stop him. At the first two websites below you can buy both the smokes and all the other smoker's accoutrements.

Accessories range from pens (no matter how many he has, the pen fairy will always have stolen most of them), braces (only if you know he wears them, of course), small leather goods, shirts, ties, cufflinks, belts, gloves and more. (It's a good idea to shop here for Christmas and birthdays too.)

Albert Thurston
www.albertthurston.com

If your dad is of the braces-wearing variety, he'll love something from this retailer (established in 1820). As well as evening and regimental collections, it stocks 'huntin' shootin' and fishin' designs, patterns and polka dots, and the unique 'Jazz' collection. Worldwide delivery.

David Hampton
www.davidhampton.com

David Hampton of London has been supplying luxury leather goods to top hotels throughout the world for the last 20 years, and now, for the first time, you can get your hands on some of their exquisitely crafted accessories online. Worldwide delivery.

Mr Pen
www.mrpen.co.uk

Mr Pen offers different ranges of pens, including Cross and Sheaffer plus the gorgeously packaged Mount Everest Legacy. An engraving service is available for most pens for a small charge and gift-wrapping is free. Ships worldwide; express UK delivery.

.

Robert Old
www.old.co.uk

Robert Old of Bournemouth offers a high quality range of men's gifts and accessories including cashmere sweaters and scarves, leather gifts from cufflink boxes to travel alarm clocks, classic English briefcases and weekenders and shoes by Crockett and Jones. They'll deliver worldwide and offer express delivery on request.

The Pen Shop
www.penshop.co.uk

This is a really attractive website offering one of the best selections of luxury pens including Yard-o-Led's beautiful sterling silver fountain pens, ballpoints and pencils, Faber Castell pens in wood and silver, Mont Blanc, and Porsche Design steel pens. They also offer Lamy, Rotring, Sheaffer and Waterman. They aim to send out on the day you order and deliver worldwide.

Simply Cigars
www.simplycigars.co.uk

This is my favourite UK-based website for cigars and humidors, as well as for very attractive accessories and gifts, wines and spirits. The cigars are expensive, as you would expect, but if you need a last minute gift for a smoker they will do their utmost to get it to you on time. Ships worldwide; express UK delivery.

Top Cubans
www.topcubans.com

Buying cigars in the UK is extremely expensive; buy from abroad, however, and you can make a huge saving. Based in Geneva, Switzerland, this company offers a wide choice, together with recommendations and advice you can trust. This site is a cigar smoker's paradise, and the worldwide delivery service is excellent.

TOILETRIES

Toiletries are an obvious answer to Father's Day gift giving: they're easy to buy, simple to send and, provided you don't try and get him to 'splash on' something new, make really excellent gifts. Find out his favourite aftershave, then buy it as cologne, soap or shower gel. Big department stores, such as Selfridges, Harvey Nichols and Harrods, are likely to sell the products; but you'll be hard put to find a better choice than offered by the stores below.

Adonis Grooming
www.adonisgrooming.com
Adonis offers an excellent range of grooming products for men including brands such as Dermalogica, Clarins for Men and Jose Eisenberg; gift accessories; travel kits by California North, Jack Black and 4V00; D R Harris fragrances and Zirh products. World-wide, UK express and gift wrapping are offered.

Carter and Bond
www.carterandbond.com
This easy-to-navigate online store is home to over 600 products from more than 40 brands, including Molton Brown, American Crew, Baxter of California, Geo F Trumper and Proraso. Whether you're looking for skin care, hair care, fragrance or shaving products you'll find them all here. Ships worldwide; express UK option.

HQ Man
www.hqman.com
If you've spent any time at all at thesiteguide.com you will already have come across wonderful hair and accessories website hqhair.com. Check out brands such as 4V00, Anthony Logistics, Calmia, Decleor Men, Malin+Goetz and Fred Bennett plus lots more, and expect to find the full ranges across body, bath, skincare, haircare and accessories. Ships worldwide; express UK option.

Jason Shankey

www.jasonshankey.co.uk

If the man in your life is a fan of American Crew, Baxters of California, Philip B or Redken for men hair treatments, this is the place for you. There's also a phenomenal range of other products on this site for both men and women from hair care and hair appliances to slimming products, men's grooming and hangover cures. Ships worldwide; express UK delivery.

Mankind

www.mankind.co.uk

This is definitely a great men's website. It's modern, easy to use and has a very good range of products on offer, showcasing the very best and most innovative shaving, skin and hair care brands – think Sean John, Remington, LAB Series and Ice – and offers them in a way that makes buying simple, fast and fun. Ships worldwide; express UK delivery plus gift wrapping.

Murdock London

www.murdocklondon.com

This modern men's grooming product retailer has produced a slick, easy-to-navigate website offering brands such as D R Harris, Caron, Malin+Goetz and Kevin Murphy, as well as aromatic candles and room scents by Mariage Frères. Ships worldwide; express UK delivery and gift boxes.

WholeMan

www.wholeman.co.uk

WholeMan is a relatively new, contemporary multi-channel men's store offering a whole range of treatments, from shaves and massages, to waxing and eyelash tinting. It also sells a wide variety of top products, including brands such as Acca Kappa, Baxter of California, Edwin Jagger and Murad. UK delivery; express option and gift wrapping.

GENERAL GIFTSTORES

The retailers below are excellent if you need a gift in a hurry, want something sent worldwide or need it wrapped for you. There's a wide choice of gift ideas on offer at all of them, so make sure you've narrowed down the kind of thing you're looking for before you visit, or you could well get sidetracked.

Bloomsbury
www.bloomsburystore.com

I particularly like the men's section here, where modern radios and iPod speakers are offered alongside fragrances by Czech & Speake, colourful accessories by Paul Smith, Bangers and Mash, Duchamp and Simon Carter, and watches by Mondaine and Opex. There are great gifts for girls here too. Ships worldwide; express UK delivery.

Harrison & Simmonds
www.h-s.co.uk

Harrison & Simmonds offer pipes, humidors, lighters, hip flasks and luxury gifts from companies such as Dalvey There is also a wide range of Mont Blanc pens (these must be ordered by phone), plus chess sets, Hunter pocket watches, shooting sticks and die-cast models of cars and aeroplanes. Ships worldwide; express UK delivery.

The Inside Man
www.theinsideman.com

There are lots of ideas for gifts for men at The Inside Man, such as art and design products, leather boxes and trays, clocks, watches, pens, stationery, smoking accessories, decanters, sports, games and toiletries. It's a really excellent men's gift department store and you're almost certain to find something suitable here. Ships worldwide; express UK delivery.express UK and gift wrapping.

WEDDINGS

Wedding gifts are a tricky subject. Most couples opt for one or even more gift lists, so you have the dilemma of choosing something from their list (and if you leave it rather late your choice can be restricted to the odd plate or even a washing-up bowl – and yes, that has happened to me) or buying something totally different.

Personally, I'm not good at buying from wedding lists as I always want to give something unique. The gifts I remember from my own wedding day are antique glasses, a wonderful modern pewter serving dish, Tiffany candle holders and the shotgun that my husband's aunt Jean gave us as a joke.

I think you should give something that you love and have chosen personally, and that suits the couple you're giving it to; which goes back to considering what kind of house they'll be living in and whether they are classic or contemporary in their style. Some people will always buy from the wedding list, while others will always do something totally different. It's up to you. How much you spend is not the point. What is the point is how much thought you've put into choosing your gift and that, frankly, is the only thing that matters.

> *'Nobody will ever win the battle of the sexes. There's too much fraternizing with the enemy.'*
> HENRY KISSINGER

I'm not going to suggest individual wedding gifts to you; everyone's choice is going to be different, but here are some very good places to buy from, both online and offline (although all have an online presence to make life easier for you).

THE DEPARTMENT STORES

The major department stores are great for china, glass, silver, linen, accessories and much more.

Harrods
www.harrods.com
See Life's Little Luxuries, page 228.

Heals
www.heals.co.uk
Heals' produces contemporary styles at reasonable prices, from major furniture items, such as beds and sofas, right through to glass and tableware, lighting, small accessories, bedlinen and towels. Express UK delivery.

John Lewis
www.johnlewis.com

The Veil
❤ **The introduction of the wedding veil stems from the time of the Crusades. In early weddings the bride was bargained for through her father; she was married wearing a veil and only revealed to her husband after the ceremony. Veils were used as a symbol of virginity and purity.**

❤ **'Veil' comes from the Latin word *velum*, which actually means 'sail'.**

Here you can find a vast range of gifts, and you might well find that the wedding couple already have their list at a branch of this store. It's a great one-stop shop, and wonderful if you don't want to buy something overpriced or very unusual. Express UK delivery and in-store gift wrapping.

CHINA, GLASS AND DECORATIVE TABLEWARE

Be careful here as the bride and groom will definitely be collecting specific types of china, glass and cutlery. The wedding list will probably give you the option of buying a few plates or place settings. Alternatively, try to buy something that isn't easy to find anywhere else. Hand-painted serving platters, beautiful hand-made bowls, glass jugs and decanters are very good single items that won't conflict with the main set. Then there are pretty dessert plates, high-quality steak knives, such as those by Laguiole, and sterling silver cake servers, perhaps by Elsa Peretti for Tiffany. These are some of the best kinds of individual gifts.

Culinary Concepts
www.culinaryconcepts.co.uk
Here you'll find some new and clever design ideas, including unusual cheese knives and servers, hammered stainless steel bowls and plates, and table accessories, such as unique sugar and olive bowls, wine buckets and vases. Ships worldwide.

Dibor
www.dibor.co.uk
Dibor is an independent, UK-based company offering French-style furniture, home accessories, tableware and glasses, plus gifts for every room, as well as the garden. Ships throughout Europe; delivery free on UK orders over £150.

Dot Maison
www.dotmaison.com
This is a beautifully designed online home store, offering a superb range of designer home furnishings and accessories by names such as Missoni, Descamps, Lulu Guinness, Jasper Conran, Versace and Vera Wang. UK delivery.

Mulberry Hall
www.mulberryhall.co.uk
Mulberry Hall offers online some of the ranges that they hold in their York shop, including brands such as Baccarat, Herend, Lladro, Royal Copenhagen and Waterford. They also offer a free gift-wrapping service, and will deliver worldwide.

Small Island Trader
www.smallislandtrader.com
Small Island Trader offers china, glass and silver from a wide range of designers, including Waterford, Villeroy & Boch and Spode. It also has kitchen equipment, from juicers to copper pots and pans, and unusual homewares. Worldwide delivery.

Thomas Goode
www.thomasgoode.co.uk
Famous for being one of the best bone china, crystal and silverware shops in the world, Thomas Goode has ranges by all the top designers, such as Royal Copenhagen, Richard Ginori, Paul Smith and Bodo Sperlein, plus Baccarat, William Yeoward and Salviati. Call to order; worldwide delivery.

Tiffany
www.tiffany.com
Take a look at their superb range of gifts. Yes, you are paying for the name, but for such a name it's worth it.
See main entry in Life's Little Luxuries, page 231.

Waterford Crystal
www.waterford.co.uk
One of the world's most beautiful collections of crystal, combining superb-quality traditional and contemporary glassware, and incorporating the work of designers such as John Rocha and Jasper Conran. Ships worldwide; offers a gift-wrapping service.

SILVERWARE AND GLASS

Silver is a lovely option to choose for a wedding present. There's plenty of choice, from traditional to modern styles, and an enormously wide range of prices. If you want to push the boat out, why not invest in something by an up-and-coming silversmith? These individuals often produce exceptional pieces that will become more precious (in every way) as time goes by. On the other hand, you can rarely go wrong with antique silver. If you go down this route, however, take care to be absolutely certain of its provenance. You should be fine on this count if you're buying through a silversmith based at the London Silver Vaults or one of the famous-name jewellers and silversmiths, but otherwise be careful. In my opinion, it's much better to give the smallest piece of sterling silver rather than anything plate, unless it's a full canteen of cutlery, of course.

Arthur Price
www.arthurprice.com

There are some very traditional silver gift ideas from this family business that was established in 1902, but there are also contemporary products by Guy Degrenne, Laurence Llewelyn-Bowen and Clive Christian. They have a wedding list service, and you can find a stock list on their website or buy from them online. Worldwide delivery.

Braybrook & Britten
www.braybrook.com

If you're looking for a really special present, just browse around this excellent online gift retailer offering hand-made British craftsman-designed silver and crystal decanters, vases and bowls, photograph frames and many more ideas. Ships worldwide; gift wrapping and express UK delivery.

Laguiole
www.laguiole-france.com

You can find parts of this wonderful French cutlery range in some cookware and department stores, but you can browse the full range online, which includes high-quality and attractive boxed sets of steak knives, cheese knives, salad servers and full canteens of cutlery. They offer worldwide delivery and an express Chrono-post service within Europe.

Langfords
www.langfords.com

The Langford family has more than seventy years' experience in silver, and was a founding member of the London Silver Vaults in the 1940s. On their website you can choose from a range of beautiful and sometimes extremely unusual pieces, which they will engrave and beautifully package for you on request. They offer worldwide delivery.

Pruden & Smith
www.silversmiths.co.uk

This really is modern silver at its best, and there's a wide range to choose from. You can't buy directly through the website at the moment, but can email or call them with your enquiry – a small price to pay for such a special range. Ships worldwide; express UK delivery available.

TJK London
www.tjklondon.com

At TJK London there's a selection of classic and contemporary silver, wood and leather gifts, including photo albums, picture frames, humidors and sterling silver Marmite and jam-jar lids. There are also really lovely glass match strikers/tealight holders with silver hallmarked collars. Ships worldwide; express UK delivery available.

ANTIQUE SILVER AND GLASS

Frank Dux Antiques

www.antique-glass.co.uk

For someone who loves beautiful glass, look no further than this website. You'll find unique alternatives to the traditional modern glass. If you need advice, simply give them a call. Worldwide delivery.

I Franks

www.ifranks.com

I Franks specialise in antique silver, and if you can't get to the Silver Vaults, this is a great place to browse their lovely collection. You can search by period (Queen Anne or George I, for example), or type of product. They ship worldwide.

Stephen Kalms

www.kalmsantiques.com

Stephen Kalms is an antique silver dealer who has managed to transfer a large proportion of his stock online in a clear and informative way. Choose the type of piece you think you might like to give, then browse what's on offer. Delivery is included in the prices quoted.

Luck and Marriage

'Something old, something new
Something borrowed, something blue
And a silver sixpence in her shoe.'

♥ **Each item in the rhyme represents a good-luck token for the bride. If all are carried or worn on her wedding day, her marriage will be lucky.**

♥ **'Something old' represents continuity with the bride's family and the past.**

♥ **'Something new' relates to optimism for the new life that lies ahead.**

♥ **'Something borrowed' is an item from a happily married friend or relative, whose good fortune in marriage will supposedly transfer to the borrower.**

♥ **'Something blue' represents purity, love, modesty and fidelity.**

♥ **Placing sixpence in the bride's shoe, a custom now largely forgotten, represents wealth and financial security. This tradition is thought to date from Victorian times.**

COOKWARE AND TOASTERS...

Oh yes, the toaster, the traditional wedding gift of yesteryear. Well, do you or don't you? Almost certainly not: they'll have put that four-slice Dualit toaster on their wedding list for sure, or they'll own one already. Two Dualit toasters? Overkill, definitely.

As far as cookware is concerned, the same applies here as it does everywhere else: buy from the wedding list or choose something 'one-off' and different. It's totally pointless duplicating something they'll almost certainly have put on their list; you might as well buy from the list yourself. To do your own thing, go somewhere like Divertimenti for decorative copper pans and bowls; Dining Store for William Bounds' Pepart salt and pepper mills; or Cucina Direct for the Gordon Ramsey Bamix.

Conran
www.conran.com
Conran are famous for their modern, colourful and well-priced furniture and accessories, which you can now buy online as well as in one of their stores. Discover their modern take on everything from kitchen accessories, candles and soft furnishings to lighting, clocks and gifts. Worldwide delivery and gift wrapping.

Cucina Direct
www.cucinadirect.co.uk
Here everything for the kitchen is beautifully displayed, including knives, pots and pans, bar tools, glasses and serving dishes, picnic equipment, housekeeping items, small electrical appliances and a gift selection. Ships worldwide; express UK delivery and gift wrapping.

'I love being married. It's so great to find that one special person you want to annoy for the rest of your life.'

RITA RUDNER

Divertimenti

www.divertimenti.co.uk

This famous London-based cookery equipment shop offers over 5000 items, from hand-painted French pottery to a really comprehensive range of kitchen essentials, including knives, boards and bakeware, Parmesan graters and ravioli trays, copper bowls and pans, and cafetières. Worldwide delivery.

> *'A man in love is incomplete until he has married. Then he's finished.'*
>
> ZSA ZSA GABOR

HOME ACCESSORIES

The main consideration in this section, if you're going to steer away from the list but get it right, is the general style of the couple who are getting married. For example, are they very traditional and going to live (or probably living already) in a cottage in the country? Are they young, fashionable, working in town and residing in a modern London Docklands' apartment? Are they going to be living abroad much of the time, and if so, where? Are they going to be cramped for space or living in a loft? You need to take all these things into account before rushing off to buy that rather expensive Royal Copenhagen Siamese cat. Absolutely beautiful it may be, but only to certain people. Don't give a gift just because you adore it; give it only if you're sure that they will as well.

Once you've considered their lifestyle, the amount of space they have and their favoured colours (chic neutrals, traditional shades, such as warm reds and blues, or stark black and white), try to find some gorgeous pieces that they'll love for ever. Spending a lot of money on the wrong thing is such a waste, and can cause embarrassment for the receiver, I'm sure you'll agree.

All the stores listed in the following pages would be very good for housewarming gifts as well.

The Dress ...

❤ Although it has long been assumed that wedding dresses were always white, that is not the case. Not until Queen Victoria married her cousin Albert of Saxe-Coburg in 1840 did white become the colour to be married in, and it has remained so ever since.

❤ In the 1849 issue of *Godey's Lady's Book*, the most successful women's magazine of its time in the USA (it had the then huge circulation of 150,000), there was the following statement about wedding attire:

'Custom has decided, from the earliest ages, that white is the most fitting hue, whatever may be the material. It is an emblem of the purity and innocence of girlhood, and the unsullied heart she now yields to the chosen one.'

❤ There is also an old poem about how the colour of your wedding dress will influence your future:

Married in white, you will have chosen all right.
Married in grey, you will go far away.
Married in black, you will wish yourself back.
Married in red, you will wish yourself dead.
Married in blue, you will always be true.
Married in pearl, you will live in a whirl.
Married in green, ashamed to be seen,
Married in yellow, ashamed of the fellow.
Married in brown, you will live out of town.
Married in pink, your spirits will sink.

LINENS AND TOWELS

If the thought of browsing for the linen cupboard makes you want to rush off and do something else, take a deep breath and have a look at the sites below. They sell not ordinary linens and towels, but the sort that are unique, that when spotted in someone else's house, you wish you owned yourself. Beautiful tablecloths and linens from France, monogrammed towels, super quality robes and hand-made American quilts are just some of the items you can find here. (If buying duvets, bedlinen or tablecloths, do make sure you know the sizes required.)

Biju
www.biju.co.uk
Luxurious bathrobes and towels, cashmere blankets (at faint-inducing prices), throws and wonderful table linen, plus tableware, mats and trays are just some of the items you can choose from on this lovely website, where they also offer enchanting children's bedding and bedroom accessories. Worldwide delivery.

Cath Kidston
www.cathkidston.co.uk
Here you'll see some really pretty and different bedlinen and bedspreads with pattern names such as 'New Bubbles' and 'Vintage Posy', plus crochet blankets and even sleeping bags. Worldwide delivery; gift wrapping and express UK delivery.

Designers Guild
www.designersguild.com
Tricia Guild offers an eclectic range of beautiful things, including home accessories, such as bedlinens and colourful towels, unique home fragrances, gorgeous blankets and cushions. These are available in her shops as well as online. Express delivery and gift wrapping is available in the UK.

The Egyptian Cotton Store
www.egyptiancottonstore.com

If you like beautiful bedlinen for yourself or to give as a gift, you'll love this attractively presented website, where you can buy top-quality Egyptian cotton duvet covers and sheets, goosedown and cotton duvets and pillows, blankets and throws, luxury towels and bathrobes, plus elegant table linen. Ships worldwide; express UK delivery and gift wrapping.

French Brand
www.french-brand.com

This is without doubt one of the best collections of bed and table linens and towels that you are likely to come across anywhere, either online or in the shops. Brands include Les Olivades, Jaquard Français, Souleido, Garnier Thiebaut, Descamps and Manuel Canovas. Worldwide delivery.

The Monogrammed Linen Shop
www.monogrammedlinenshop.co.uk

For the past twenty-five years, the Monogrammed Linen Shop has provided classical and contemporary household linens to customers from all over the world. They use the most beautiful laces and embroideries, together with the finest cottons, linens and silks to produce luxurious bedlinen, table linen and nightwear. Worldwide delivery.

Olde Glory
www.oldeglory.co.uk

Having spent a great deal of time in the USA, I've become really attached to the old-style quilts, wall hangings, Shaker boxes and cushions that are part and parcel of the American country look. For that reason I'm delighted to have found this lovely website, which offers hand-made quilts in a variety of colourways. Ships worldwide.

Purple & Fine Linen

www.purpleandfinelinen.co.uk

Pure linen tablecloths, placemats, napkins and runners designed to offer a look of timeless luxury and simple elegance are on offer at this website, as well as linen in traditional white and ivory. You can also choose from their range in deep chilli red and damson (purple), which would be lovely for Christmas, plus black and chocolate brown. The company ships worldwide; express delivery within the UK.

Volga Linen

www.volgalinen.co.uk

Volga Linen is a family-run British company that sells an exquisite array of pure linen from Russia and Europe. The collection consists of table linen in plain and fancy damasks, bedlinen, bed covers and throws, hand towels and accessories. As a gift, I'd suggest buying their damask table napkins, which are designed to last for years. Ships worldwide; express UK delivery. Gift wrapping and monogramming available.

ALBUMS AND JOURNALS

Albumania

www.albumania.com

At Albumania you design your own photo album, box file, guest book, wine book, address book or diary. Just download a photograph, choose the colour of binding and ribbon, all online and then see exactly what the cover of your book will look like. Worldwide delivery and gift boxing.

Aspinal of London

www.aspinaloflondon.com

See page 218.

ANNIVERSARIES

I always marvel when I hear about people celebrating their golden wedding anniversary. Fifty years! With the same person. Wonderful – I hope.

You tend to start hearing about how long people have been together when they celebrate their twenty-fifth, or silver, anniversary. Yes, couples and families might celebrate the day in previous years, but when do you hear of someone having a party for their sixth or sixteenth wedding anniversary? Never, really.

My husband, Andrew, and I have a competition to see who remembers our anniversary first. I nearly always win. Last year we had been married for twenty years and we celebrated by going somewhere lovely. The year before Andrew was on his tractor in the garden, cutting the grass (that probably sounds strange, but it's another story and I'm not going to tell you about it now). I went up to him and said 'Happy anniversary'. Needless to say, he was a) not very pleased that I'd taken him by surprise, and b) furious that there was little he could do about it. You can't just suddenly leap off a tractor, rush into the house and come out with a card and some flowers, now can you? I made him pay for that one. Another year, I have to confess, we both forgot. Oh, dear – we've obviously been married too long. Anyway, I think that every anniversary is worth celebrating with flowers at least. Are you listening, dear?

ANNIVERSARY GIFT LIST

Year	UK	US	Modern
1st	Paper	Paper	Clocks
2nd	Cotton	Cotton	China
3rd	Leather	Leather	Crystal
4th	Fruit/Flowers	Linen/Silk	Appliances
5th	Wood	Wood	Silverware
6th	Sugar	Iron	Wood
7th	Wool/Copper	Wool/Copper	Desk Sets
8th	Bronze/Pottery	Bronze	Linen/Lace
9th	Pottery/Willow	Pottery	Leather
10th	Tin	Tin/Aluminium	Diamond Jewels
11th	Steel	Steel	Fashion jewellery
12th	Silk/Linen	Silk/Linen	Pearls
13th	Lace	Lace	Textiles/Furs
14th	Ivory	Ivory	Gold Jewellery
15th	Crystal	Crystal	Watches
20th	China	China	Platinum
25th	Silver	Silver	Silver
30th	Pearl	Pearl	Diamond
35th	Coral	Coral/Jade	Jade
40th	Ruby	Ruby	Ruby
45th	Sapphire	Sapphire	Sapphire
50th	Gold	Gold	Gold
55th	Emerald	Emerald	Emerald
60th	Diamond	Diamond	Diamond

Most people are familiar with the traditional anniversary materials list, although many would now be a bit challenging to convert into really thoughtful gifts. Parts of the traditional list have been in existence since medieval times, with historians tracing the origins of silver and gold anniversaries to medieval Germany, where couples were presented with garlands made of these metals for their 25th and 50th years of marriage.

The rest of the 'traditional' list didn't exist until 1937, when the American National Retail Jeweler Association published a list associating a material for each anniversary up to the 15th, and then for every fifth year after that, up to the 60th.

It was probably after Queen Victoria celebrated her 60th year on the throne, the 'Diamond Jubilee', that diamonds came to be associated with sixty years. They are also associated with seventy-five years.

As the modern list is much more specific, you'll find it easier to buy gifts that match the appropriate year. I'm not sure that anyone would appreciate a gift made of tin, even if you could find one. In any case, you're far more likely to be involved in other people's anniversaries once they reach their silver wedding, where the choice becomes easier in some ways – silver is silver, after all – and harder in others – just how much do you want to spend?

One morning in the summer of 1950, Billy Wilder was sitting alone, eating breakfast and reading the 'Hollywood Reporter'. His wife, Audrey, came into the room and asked: 'Do you know what day this is, dear?' 'June 30th.' 'It's our anniversary.' 'Please,' Wilder said, 'not while I'm eating.'

TRADITIONS ACROSS THE WORLD

💜 **In the UK you can receive a congratulatory message from the Queen for 60th, 65th and 70th wedding anniversaries, and any anniversary after that. This is done by applying to Buckingham Palace.**

💜 **In the United States you can receive a greeting from the President for any wedding anniversary after the 50th.**

💜 **In Australia you can receive a letter of congratulations from the Governor General and the Prime Minister on your 60th wedding anniversary.**

You can, of course, stick to the gift list on page 82 and find something that works with the relevant year. I personally think, particularly if you're going to quite a large celebration, that it's better to think of something both appropriate and a bit different (I always seem to be saying that). Take into account the year's material, either traditional or modern. Then consider the couple's overall style. I think you've probably got the message by now, so take a look at the suggestions on the following pages. Also take a look at the gift stores in the wedding section (page 66), where there are lots of ideas suitable for all anniversaries. I have picked specific gifts only for silver, ruby and gold anniversaries as these are the ones you're most likely to be invited to help celebrate.

When choosing gifts for any wedding anniversary remember to take into account the couple's ages. Some people get married very early and celebrate their silver wedding in their late forties; others will be quite a bit older. This too will define what you choose to give.

Abstract Bottles

www.abstractbottles.com

If you don't want to give silver/rubies/diamonds, but you do want to give something different and original, take a look at this website, where you can create and design your own bespoke bottle online, incorporating your personalised message. UK delivery and gift wrapping.

Coast Interiors

www.coastinteriors.com

This is a lovely, clearly designed, online interiors store offering a very good range for the home, from luxury bath towels and cutlery canteens to throws, cushions, fine china and candle holders. Particularly good is their selection of crystal and silver. EU express delivery, engraving and gift wrapping.

Distinctly British

www.distinctlybritish.com

Two of my favourites here for anniversary presents are the cranberry glasses from Exmoor Glass, which would be excellent for a ruby wedding celebration, and the My House History Portfolio, which provides a personalised dossier tracing the history of a home and property and includes an aerial photograph. Worldwide delivery available.

The Drink Shop

www.thedrinkshop.com

Bols Gold is a liqueur dating back to the time of Louis XIV and would make an unusual golden wedding gift. The pieces of genuine 24-carat gold leaf floating in the liqueur are part of its ancient tradition. For silver weddings consider Veuve Clicquot Vintage Rich 2002 with its silver label, or a bottle of Patron Silver Tequila, neither of which you'll find easily elsewhere. EU delivery and UK express available.

Frank Dux Antiques
www.antique-glass.co.uk
See page 73.

Halcyon Days
www.halcyon-days.co.uk
Here you'll find hand-painted enamel boxes with a wide variety of designs, including flowers, animals and pretty patterns, which can be customised with dates, names and messages. They also sell musical boxes (one of which plays 'The Anniversary Waltz'), porcelain figures of characters from *The Wind in the Willows*, jewelled boxes, clocks and many other gift ideas. Worldwide delivery, gift wrap and express delivery.

Historic Newspapers
www.historic-newspapers.co.uk
This is a terrific site at which you can order genuine original newspapers (not copies) dating back over 200 years that have been preserved in an historic newspaper archive. You start by selecting a presentation folder or gift box, then the date and the newspaper of your choice, after which you can personalise the certificate of authenticity. Worldwide, express delivery and presentation boxes and folders.

The Gift Experience
www.thegiftexperience.co.uk
There's one idea in particular here that would make a really lovely gift for any anniversary – an etched glass photo frame. You'll need to find a photograph of the couple who are celebrating and upload it (or scan and upload). Then the company will engrave the glass and put your message underneath. Worldwide and UK express delivery for non-personalised items.

The Pier

www.pier.co.uk

The Pier always offers a wide range of interesting objects, including, for example, glass and gold leaf vases, Baroque-style gold candlesticks, blue and silver canapé (or butter) knives, silver leaf photo frames – into which you could put a picture, of course – mosaic-framed mirrors, exotic tapestries and jewel-coloured quilts. It's a real treasure trove. UK delivery.

TWO MORE IDEAS FOR YOU

The following ideas will both take you a bit more time than buying something online, but will be well worth the effort.

The Photo Album

Buy a really beautiful, large photo album from www.aspinaloflondon.com or www.circalondon.co.uk. Collect together all the pictures you have of the couple (and ask their children and friends as well) and create an album to commemorate their anniversary, be it silver, ruby or gold. Needless to say the longer they've been married, the more pictures of family, children, grandchildren, parties and other celebrations you'll be able to find. What you can do is re-create a virtual history of their life together. This gift is always a huge success.

The Planter

For this you can take a look at the planters/large decorated bowls (preferably hand-painted) available at www.in2decor.com or at a department store near you. You can tailor your choice of planter to the couple's style, then take it along to your local florist and have it filled with seasonal plants that will last a while. I have done this on several occasions, using orchids (my favourites) and a selection of other beautiful plants.

NEW BABY CELEBRATIONS

*I*t's traditional to buy a gift for a new baby – but then you knew that, didn't you? Nowadays there are lots of places where you can find wonderful, pretty and innovative gifts. You can storm the shops, of course, as soon as you get the announcement, or you can order online, which to me (unsurprisingly) is much the easiest option.

CHRISTENINGS

The New Testament gives several accounts of baptisms performed in the River Jordan by John the Baptist and various disciples of Jesus. The earliest known written instructions for baptism appear in an anonymous book called *The Didache, or Teaching of the Twelve Apostles,* which most scholars date to some time in the first half of the 2nd century.

Most Christians baptise their babies either by pouring or sprinkling water on the infants' heads. Some Eastern Orthodox and Roman Catholic traditions baptise their babies by totally immersing them in the font.

Baptism
Collins Dictionary *defines the word 'baptism' as follows: 1 (Christianity) to immerse (a person) in water or sprinkle water on (him or her) as part of the rite of baptism; 2 to give a name to.*

I'm a huge believer in avoiding traditional christening gifts of the napkin ring/feeder variety and would recommend looking for beautiful things that will be used later on. It's very tempting to go for that pretty hand-painted baby china, but you can be absolutely sure that by the time the baby is old enough to appreciate it, the various pieces will have been broken, lost, or still be in their box at the back of a cupboard. A pretty silver pendant or bracelet, a painting or frame, an individual, modern piece of silver, such as a tumbler or tankard, that can be displayed at home – all make wonderful gifts. There's no question in my mind that the pair of gold cufflinks given to my younger son will always be his favourite christening present. He might forget why he was given them, but he'll never forget the giver and will wear them for ever.

Aspinal of London
www.aspinaloflondon.com
See the full entry in Last-Minute Lifesavers (page 218).
Look here for beautiful photo albums and keepsake boxes.

Berry Brothers & Rudd
www.bbr.com
See the full entry in Champagne and Wine (page 210).
Consider starting a Cellar Plan here if you're feeling very generous, or lay down some port that the child can drink with you at a later date – perhaps their 21st birthday. (And make absolutely sure that the parents know it's not for drinking now.)

Hickory Dickory
www.hickorydickory.co.uk
Hickory Dickory sells enchanting hand-made children's room accessories, including mobiles, height charts, name plates, clocks and mirrors, all of which can be personalised with a name or date. The clocks are always a success. Allow 2–3 weeks for delivery and call them for urgent or overseas orders.

The Little Present Company

www.littlepresentcompany.co.uk

A hammered silver bowl, Armada dish, or horn and silver bon-bon dish are just some of the christening gift ideas you can find here. UK delivery, UK express and engraving are available.

Marie Chantal

www.mariechantal.com

If you really can't resist buying some gorgeous babywear, take a look at this exquisite collection designed by Marie Chantal of Greece. Nothing is inexpensive but everything will be bound to raise a smile - from the parents, at least. Worldwide delivery.

Nursery Window

www.nurserywindow.co.uk

Nursery Window has a gorgeous range of baby blankets in cashmere and lambswool which would make lovely gifts. At time of writing there are checks, plains and rabbit-festooned varieties, to choose from, with fringes and satin edges.

Richmond Silver

www.richmondsilver.co.uk

Reasonably priced candlesticks and modern crystal decanters are just some of the items you can choose from here, plus unusual silver and gemstone pendants and a good range of cufflinks. UK delivery, engraving, gift wrapping and express delivery.

Tiffany

www.tiffany.com

Christening gifts here range from the reasonable to the totally fantastical and include frames, combs and keepsake boxes. My advice? Choose an Elsa Peretti silver heart pendant for a girl and she'll thank you for evermore. If it's a boy, you could buy a pair of silver 'Return to Tiffany New York' cufflinks.

BABY SHOWERS AND NEW ARRIVALS

Baby showers are parties where new mothers, expectant or otherwise, receive gifts for their baby. It is an American tradition that is becoming more and more popular in Europe. In the UK this is a girls-only event, although in the USA baby showers are held for both parents (and there are even men-only showers). They're also held in Africa, Asia, Latin America and the Middle East. In India, religious rituals similar to modern baby showers are held during the seventh month of pregnancy.

Traditionally, the shower is hosted and arranged by someone other than the mother, preferably a friend rather than a relative. Baby-themed games, favours and 'tummy rubbing' are the order of the day. I'll admit now that when I had my three children, quite a few years ago, baby showers had not made it across the pond. Gifts for the baby? Wonderful. Tummy rubbing? No, I don't think so, but then that's just me. You might think it marvellous.

Godparents

Traditionally, godparents are responsible for their godchildren's religious education and supposed to care for them should they be orphaned. In modern times this has changed somewhat, and the emphasis is more on influencing upbringing and development. Being asked to be a godparent is a compliment, but it has no legal status unless special arrangements are made.

In the Anglican Church each child is given three godparents, two of the same sex and one of the opposite sex. To qualify they must have been baptised themselves. In the Catholic Church you can become a godparent only if you have been confirmed.

Babas

www.babas.uk.com

All of Babas' beautiful hand-made baby bedding and accessories are individually made for you and wrapped in their own unique calico packaging. You can choose sets for cribs, cots and Moses baskets, or sleeping bags and towels in their range of contemporary designs with names such as Noah's Ark, Teddy Triplets and Splashy Duck. Worldwide delivery and gift wrapping.

'Before I got married, I had six theories about bringing up children. Now I have six children and no theories.'

JOHN WILMOT,
EARL OF ROCHESTER

Babes with Babies

www.babeswithbabies.com

This is definitely a lovely place to buy a gift for a new mum or babe. Here you will find pretty polka-dot mama and baby pyjamas, chic nursing tops, superfluffy alpaca slippers, pampering gift sets and incredibly elegant baby bags, plus lots of ideas for babies. Worldwide delivery and free gift wrapping.

Baby Celebrate

www.babycelebrate.co.uk

This is a Cheshire-based baby gift retailer where there are delightful ideas for newborn and slightly older babies, such as Baby Play Basket and Luxury Baby on the Go. For slightly older children, they have pretty printed cutlery sets and lunch boxes, plus colourful soft and wooden toys. Worldwide delivery, express UK and gift wrapping.

Baby Gift Box

www.babygiftbox.co.uk

The Baby Gift Box Company offers a really lovely range of ideas. You can choose from Welcome Home baby boxes with names such as Flower Power and Lullaby, soft lambswool or fleece and cashmere blankets, hand-embroidered babygrows and lots more. There's also the Yummy Mummy Gift Set to ensure that the new mum isn't forgotten. UK and express delivery plus gift wrapping.

Baby Gift Gallery
www.babygiftgallery.co.uk
The range of baby gifts on offer at this attractive website is huge, so be prepared to take your time. In particular, take a look at the Flower Stork baby bouquets, Powell & Craft quilts, Doudou et Compagnie House of Barbotine Gift Boxes, and Bob & Blossom babywear. Worldwide delivery, express UK and gift wrapping.

Bellini Baby
www.bellini-baby.com
Bellini Baby offers you the opportunity to buy absolutely beautiful baskets and hampers (most of which include champagne, so they're for you too), Takinou of France soft toys, Bébé-Jou soft cotton terry baby dressing gowns, pampering essentials and chocolates. All are gorgeously wrapped and hand-tied with ribbon. Worldwide delivery, express UK and gift wrapping.

Boutique to You
www.boutiquetoyou.co.uk
Boutique to You specialise in personalised gifts, gadgets and jewellery perfect for lots of different occasions. They've introduced some cult jewellery brands from the USA, including Mummy & Daddy Tags, Lisa Goodwin New York, and Fairy Tale Jewels. Worldwide delivery and gift wrapping.

FuzzyBuzzys
www.fuzzybuzzys.co.uk
Fuzzybuzzys create personalised fleece blankets for babies, made from the softest lambskin fleece and 100 per cent double-brushed

cotton. The blankets are machine washable, quick-dry and colour-fast. You choose from their range of colours, prints and appliqués, then personalise your blanket with the baby's name. EU delivery and gift wrapping.

JojoMamanBébé
www.jojomamanbebe.co.uk
This is a pretty store offering a very good choice for babies and young children. The drop-down menus on the home page take you quickly and clearly to everything you might be looking for, whether it's baby essentials, nightwear, towelling snugglers or their range of gifts. Worldwide delivery and gift wrapping.

The Baby
www.thebaby.co.uk
Click on the 'Treat Me' section for enchanting babygrows, hats, unusual rocking chairs and delightful toys; or the 'Care for Me' section for stylish changing bags or the Bloom Coco lounger. There's a really great choice. Worldwide delivery, UK express and gift wrapping.

Passionleaf
www.passionleaf.com
Passionleaf create amazing, real fruit bouquets, using strawberries, melons, oranges and pineapples cut into pretty shapes and packed into wicker tubs. Just looking at this website will make your mouth water. You can also add balloons and chocolate strawberries to your gift. Call to order. They currently deliver mainly in the M25 area but this is expanding so check. Express delivery available.

'When the first baby laughed for the first time, the laugh broke into a thousand pieces and they all went skipping about, and that was the beginning of fairies.'

J.M. BARRIE, *PETER PAN*

HOUSEWARMING CELEBRATIONS

R alph Richardson did more than warm the house when he visited his friends Vivien Leigh and Laurence Olivier. Richardson took fireworks to their first housewarming in Chelsea to set off in their small backyard. He lit the largest one first, but instead of it shooting upwards, it zoomed through open windows into the dining room, burned up the curtains and set the cornice ablaze. Vivien Leigh was not amused.

Some years later, the Oliviers invited Richardson and his wife to another of their homes: Notley Abbey. After dinner Olivier invited Richardson to see the paintings in the attic created by the medieval monks who had previously owned the abbey. A short while later there was a cry and a loud crash. The women rushed upstairs to discover Richardson on the bed in the main guestroom, surrounded by dust and plaster, with a gaping hole above him. Richardson had stepped back between the rafters and had fallen through the ceiling.

May your troubles be less, And your blessing be more. And nothing but happiness, Come through your door

IRISH BLESSING.

You probably won't want to spend a fortune on a housewarming gift, so here is a list of retailers with a range of prices. Some are luxury and some are not. I'm not going to go down the 'think of the couple and work out their style' road again – I think you've heard that from me enough. Take your pick.

Alison Henry

www.alisonhenry.com

This retailer offers seriously gorgeous modern accessories, mainly in neutral colours, which would make superb gifts for 'important' occasions, or when you feel in need of adding something really special to your home. UK delivery.

Bodie and Fou

www.bodieandfou.com

The Bodie and Fou collection of European designer home accessories includes unique and stylish interior decor, kitchenware, lighting and chic French homeware alongside gift ideas such as Normann Copenhagen cognac glasses, ceramic lamps and crystal carafes. Worldwide and UK express delivery.

Brissi

www.brissi.co.uk

Although many of the products on offer at this home accessories store have a retro feel, the overall mood is chic and modern, with beautiful photography and mainly neutral colours. The range includes crystal perfume bottles, black and white Limoges tableware and classic glass. They offer worldwide and express delivery.

Coffee & Cream

www.coffeeandcream.co.uk

This attractive website offers unusual home accessories: animal print candles, faux fur throws, black ceramic canisters, smoky glasses and pale French Provençal cushions. Worldwide delivery.

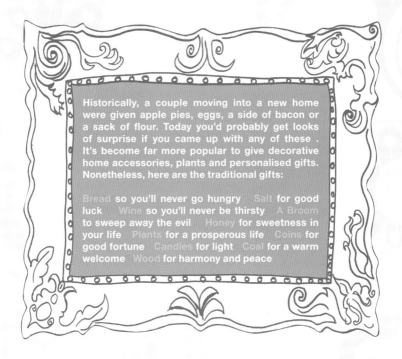

Historically, a couple moving into a new home were given apple pies, eggs, a side of bacon or a sack of flour. Today you'd probably get looks of surprise if you came up with any of these . It's become far more popular to give decorative home accessories, plants and personalised gifts. Nonetheless, here are the traditional gifts:

Bread so you'll never go hungry   Salt for good luck   Wine so you'll never be thirsty   A Broom to sweep away the evil   Honey for sweetness in your life   Plants for a prosperous life   Coins for good fortune   Candles for light   Coal for a warm welcome   Wood for harmony and peace

Lavender & Sage
www.lavenderandsage.co.uk

Lavender & Sage offer you a beautiful and high-quality range, including items such as attractive mirrors and wall clocks, French tableware and glass, 'Grand Hotel' luxury towels, traditional bedlinen and unusual lanterns. Just about everything here would make lovely gift. Worldwide delivery.

Lytton & Lily
www.lyttonandlily.co.uk

There is so much to see here that you almost don't know where to start: colourful enamelware; Cath Kidston china and bistro cutlery; Comptoire Grande towels, bedlinens and throws; candles, clocks and mirrors, and a great deal more. Worldwide delivery, express UK and gift wrapping.

HOUSEWARMING TRADITIONS

France: *Friends are usually invited to a party, which is called 'pendre la crémaillère' (hang the hook rack). In the Middle Ages the crémaillère, which was built into the chimney and used for hanging kettles and cooking pots over the fire, was the last thing to be fixed in the house. Once it was hung, a meal could be cooked to thank whoever had helped with the building of the house. These days guests usually bring a present for the house.*

Russia: *Gifts of bread and salt, an old Russian folk custom, were the tradition here. When the emperor and empress paid a visit to a village, merchants and gentry would present them with a round loaf of bread piled with salt as a sign of hospitality. The bread represents good health and the salt long life.*

Germany/Switzerland: *Bread and salt are also given in Germany and parts of Switzerland, the idea being that they give you strength and scare away anything bad. Salt is scattered around the house, or anywhere where the devil or his companions could be a bad influence. In the old days bread and salt were also hung up in stables to frighten the witches away, and in a new house to keep the new inhabitants safe from hunger. These days you can ask the baker in advance to bake a special 'housewarming' bread.*

India: *For the people living in West Bengal, 'sani-satyanarayan puja' is a must, and smashing a coconut before entering a new home is supposed to be good luck. In some parts of India housewarming is called 'Grihaprabesha'. In the Tamil calendar the fourth month of the year is considered inauspicious, so no housewarming traditions are held during that time.*

Nina Campbell

www.ninacampbell.com

As you would expect, the website of well-known interior designer Nina Campbell is beautifully designed. Choose from a range of her home accessories, including Limoges china, hand-made glass bonbon bowls, coloured goblets, linens, patterned lambswool throws and decorative items, such as match strikers and lacquer frames. Worldwide delivery.

Oka

www.okadirect.com

Oka offers some inspirational ideas for home gifts. Browse through their room-sets and pick out the individual items you like. From throws, cushions, quilts and rugs to porcelain vases and elegant furniture, there's a wealth of items to choose from. There's also the Rapt gift service, offering decorative accessories from the stores all beautifully wrapped (of course) in tasselled gift boxes. Worldwide delivery.

Polly Online

www.polly-online.co.uk

Here you will find an eclectic, contemporary collection. Unusual sculptures and modern jewellery sit alongside funky lighting, 'sculpted' cushions and pretty, reasonably priced sets of tableware, making this a good place for wedding gifts, as well as for other occasions. Worldwide delivery and gift wrapping.

Pretty Practicals

www.prettypracticals.co.uk

This delightfully designed website is home to a range of beautiful interior and garden accessories, such as decorative mirrors, pretty storage boxes, candles in flowered glasses, figurines, toile de jouy quilts, and unusual clocks. Ships worldwide.

CHRISTMAS

*T*here is so much religion, history, folklore and tradition surrounding Christmas that it is impossible to include it all here. While writing this I've found out so much I didn't know before. Let me start by saying that there are two things you should do. First, buy yourself a copy of Clement C. Moore's absolutely enchanting *'Twas the Night before Christmas* (Houghton Mifflin, 2005), then decide how many you're going to buy to give away next year. Second, take a look at 'Downsizing Christmas', which you'll find at www.ahajokes.com. It's too long to reproduce here, but full of dry humour and wit – I love it.

I'm not going to give you lots of ideas for Christmas gifts here because this whole book is about gift giving. If you follow my 'golden rules' on how to choose a present, you'll know what to get and where to look. Remember always to think about the style, taste, outlook and lifestyle of the person you're buying for. Tie that down and you won't go wrong. Just make sure you don't leave your Christmas shopping until the last minute.

'Twas the night before Christmas, when all through the house
Not a creature was stirring, not even a mouse;
The stockings were hung by the chimney with care,
In hopes that St Nicholas soon would be there.

CLEMENT C MOORE, 'A VISIT FROM ST NICHOLAS'

Plan to sit down a few weeks before the 25th and make your list, using the information you have gathered about your friends and family.

Look through the Gift Lists section (page 112) to see what to buy for people with specific interests, then consider the wonderful shopping places in the Gift Essentials section (page 188), from food and drink to fashion and jewels.

And finally... visit my favourite places to find Christmas goodies for use at home or to give away.

EAT, DRINK AND BE MERRY

Whether you want to buy a side of smoked salmon to take with you to friends at Christmas, give a beautifully decorated Christmas cake as a gift, or find the best Christmas pudding on the market, they're all listed here at my favourite Christmas speciality stores.

CAKES AND COOKIES
Bettys by Post
www.bettysbypost.co.uk
Christmas cakes, speciality breads and confectionery are. just some of the temptations on offer here. Worldwide delivery.

Biscuiteers
www.biscuiteers.com
Pretty gift tins of Christmas cookies in traditional and original shapes, such as shoes and handbags. UK delivery.

Meg Rivers
www.megrivers.com
Chocolate cakes, prettily iced Christmas cakes and amazing chocolate brownies are offered here. Worldwide delivery and gift wrapping.

The Christmas Cake
www.thechristmascake. com
The Edmiston sisters make wonderful-looking Christmas cakes based on an old family recipe. UK delivery.

TURKEYS AND MORE

Blackface Farm
www.blackface.co.uk
Turkeys, game, venison and more.

Franklins Farm
www.franklinsfarm.co.uk
Free-range geese, turkeys and ducks.

Graig Farm
www.graigfarm.co.uk
Organic turkeys, meat, game.

Kelly Turkeys
www.kelly-turkeys.com
Award-winning exclusive breed of KellyBronze turkeys.

CHEESES

Paxton & Whitfield
www.paxtonandwhitfield.co.uk
Wonderful cheese, hams, chutneys and more (plus vouchers). Ships worldwide; express UK delivery.

The Cheese Society
www.thecheesesociety.co.uk
Specialist European cheeses and gift selections. Ships worldwide; express UK delivery.

Fromages
www.fromages.com
Superb French cheeses. Worldwide express delivery.

Neal's Yard Dairy
www.nealsyarddairy.co.uk
Cheese selections and Colston Basset Stilton. UK delivery.

Christmas Stockings

The tradition of giving gifts in a stocking at Christmas goes back to a time when Dutch children filled their clogs with straw and left them by the fireplace for the reindeer or donkeys of St Nicholas. He would leave them little treats as a thank you. Over time, the clogs became socks and the socks became stockings.

The Holly and the Ivy

Early Christians used to display evergreen plants in their homes to symbolise everlasting life. Holly (representing the masculine) and ivy (the feminine) were the most popular combination.

Christmas Crackers

When a confectioner's apprentice from London called Tom Smith visited Paris in 1840, he saw sugared almond bonbons wrapped in coloured tissue paper, and was very taken with them. On his return to England, he tried to introduce them to British public, but they did not prove to be as popular as he had hoped. As a result, he tried to develop them into something more exciting. Watching the logs in his fireplace crackle and spark one evening inspired him to create a bonbon with a pop. He also included mottoes and poems. These became Christmas crackers.

SMOKED FISH

Galloway Smokehouse

www.gallowaysmokehouse.co.uk

Prize-winning smoked salmon, trout, seafood and game. Ships worldwide; UK express.

Skye Seafood

www.skye-seafood.co.uk

Scottish smoked salmon, shellfish and selection boxes. Ships worldwide; UK express.

Inverawe Smokehouse

www.smokedsalmon.co.uk

Smoked Wild Atlantic salmon, plus gifts, hampers and gourmet boxes, beef and pies, shortbread and fruit cakes, pickles, chutneys, jellies and cheeses. EU delivery; express UK.

The Organic Smokehouse

www.organicsmokehouse.com

Organic smoked salmon, chicken, butter, brie and olive oil. Worldwide delivery.

Santa

Santa Claus, derived from the Dutch name for St Nicholas, is also known as Father Christmas, Kris Kringle, Père Noel, Babbo Natale, Weihnachtsmann and Father Frost.

Santa, as we think of him now, was created largely by the works of Clement Clark Moore and the cartoonist Thomas Nast. Dr Moore from New York wrote his poem 'A Visit from St Nicholas' in 1822 to read to his children on Christmas Eve. It was eventually sent without his consent to the *New York Sentinel,* which published it, and it then became extremely popular. Thomas Nast drew a new Santa image annually from 1863 for *Harper's Weekly* and is credited with creating much of his current image.

HAMS AND DELI PRODUCTS

Carluccios

www.carluccios.com

Olive oils, pasta, gift boxes and more.

Dukeshill

www.dukeshillham.co.uk

Hams, cured meats, terrines and smoked salmon.

'The one thing women don't want to find in their stockings on Christmas morning is their husband.'

JOAN RIVERS

Forman & Field

www.formanandfield.com

Hams, cheeses, smoked fish, game, deli items and more. UK delivery.

London Fine Foods

www.efoodies.co.uk

Foie gras, truffles, caviar and much more. UK and express delivery.

Valvona & Crolla

www.valvonacrolla-online. co.uk

Superb Italian delicatessen. Prosciutto, cheeses and many traditional treats for Christmas. UK and express delivery.

SOME THINGS YOU REALLY OUGHT TO KNOW ABOUT CHRISTMAS...

✳ The word 'Christmas' is a contraction of 'Christ's Mass', a phrase first recorded in 1038, which refers to the Mass said to celebrate Christ's birth.

✳ Christmas is sometimes shortened to Xmas because the Greek letter X (*chi*) has been used as an abbreviation for 'Christ' since the mid-16th century.

✳ Christmas was banned in 1647 by England's Puritan rulers following the Civil War. Riots broke out in several cities. The Restoration of 1660 ended the ban.

✳ In the USA the New England Puritans disapproved of Christmas, and it was outlawed in Boston from 1659 to 1681. However, it was still celebrated in the states of Virginia and New York.

✳ Christmas fell out of favour after the American Revolution, being viewed as an 'English custom'. The short stories of Washington Irving helped revive interest in the 1820s.

Christmas Cards

In 1843 a British civil servant called Henry Cole commissioned his friend John Calcott Horsley, a well-known artist, to design a card containing the message 'A Merry Christmas and a Happy New Year' that he could send to friends. It was so popular that it was produced commercially and became the first mass-produced Christmas card.

CHOCOLATE HEAVEN

Brownes
www.brownes.co.uk
Hand-made truffles and truffle crackers. Worldwide delivery.

Cocoa Loco
www.cocoaloco.co.uk
Beautifully packaged organic truffles and chocolate brownies. Ships worldwide; express UK delivery.

Green & Blacks
www.greenandblacksdirect.com
Beautifully packaged organic chocolate at a reasonable price. Offers bespoke gift boxes. UK delivery; express on request.

Montezumas
www.montezumas.co.uk
Wonderful chocolate truffles and gift boxes, plus exceptional chocolate buttons. Ships worldwide; express UK delivery.

COFFEE AND TEA

Fortnum & Mason
www.fortnumandmason.com
Wonderfully packaged teas and coffees. Worldwide delivery.

The Bean Shop
www.thebeanshop.com
High-quality tea and coffee, plus gift selections. UK, EU and USA delivery.

Whittard of Chelsea
www.whittard.co.uk
Excellent teas and coffees, and great gift ideas. Worldwide delivery.

Mistletoe
From the earliest times mistletoe has been one of the most magical and sacred plants of European folklore. Believed to bestow life and fertility, it was used to protect against poison and act as an aphrodisiac. In the Middle Ages branches of mistletoe were hung from ceilings to ward off evil spirits, and in Europe they were placed over house and stable doors to prevent witches entering. In some parts of England the Christmas mistletoe is burnt on Twelfth Night (see page 110) lest all the boys and girls who have kissed under it never marry.

CHRISTMAS PUDDINGS
Fortnum & Mason
www.fortnumandmason.com

Traditional luxury puddings in a range of sizes. Ships to many countries.

Georgie Porgie's Puddings
www.georgieporgies puddings.co.uk

These puds include raisins, orange peel, brandy, rum and spices, and serve from one person up to 15. UK delivery.

The Carved Angel
www.thecarvedangel.com

The Carved Angel's renowned Christmas puddings are sold in earthenware bowls tied with satin ribbon. Must be ordered early; available in three sizes. UK delivery.

The Three Wise Men

Medieval tradition has it that the names of the Three Wise Men were Balthazar, Caspar and Melchior. Where they came from is not known. They are not described, named or numbered in the Bible, where they are called Magi, or Wise Men. The idea that they were kings developed in the Middle Ages, and was based on Biblical prophecies about kings bearing gifts.

'I once bought my kids a set of batteries for Christmas with a note on it saying, "Toys not included".'

BERNARD MANNING

Twelfth Night and the Christmas Cake

Twelfth Night is the evening of 5 January and has been celebrated as the end of the Christmas season since the Middle Ages. A 'Twelfth cake' was made for the celebrations, which became more and more elaborate over the years, and was the forerunner of today's Christmas cake.

The Yule Log

In medieval times a large log, often decorated with greenery and ribbon, was ceremoniously carried into the house on Christmas Eve, and put in the fireplace of the main communal room. It was lit with the saved end of the previous year's log and burnt continuously for the Twelve Days of Christmas.

The Christmas Tree

The tradition of having a decorated tree in the house at Christmas comes from Germany (although the very first Christmas tree might well have originated in Latvia), and was introduced to England during the Georgian period. Queen Victoria and Prince Albert made decorated trees a focal point for their festivities each year. It was usual for the tree to be placed in a pot and displayed on a table. Decorated with wax candles, baskets of sweets, little ornaments and flags, it had gifts placed underneath.

ALL THE EXTRAS
Lakeland

www.lakelandlimited.co.uk

Turkish delight, candied fruits, marrons glace, spiced nuts and much more. Worldwide delivery and express UK.

For ideas on what to drink and where to buy, please see the entries in the Champagne and Wine section, page 210.

'If I could work my will,' said Scrooge indignantly, 'every idiot who goes about with "Merry Christmas" upon his lips should be boiled with his own pudding, and buried with a stake of holly through his heart.'

CHARLES DICKENS,
A CHRISTMAS CAROL

2 THE GIFT LISTS

ADVENTURER

*M*ost of us know an adventurous type whom we can imagine getting up to extreme exploits. Maybe you have one lurking in your family. Whether male or female, this person is the type that will be off 'at the drop of a hat' to explore a new country, climb a mountain, take the kids hiking in Vietnam, ski down a mountain with a two-year old strapped to their back, or be willing to pitch a tent while you're huddled in front of the fire with a mug of hot cocoa. Basically, they are up for just about anything. They are not always easy to spot – you might only come across them besuited in their normal working habitat – but once you've recognised the type, buying for them is a breeze.

Digital Hero camera
www.actioncameras.co.uk
This 3 megapixel wrist-strap action camera – waterproof to a depth of 30 metres – is also a video camera that can shoot 54 minutes in colour and with sound. Apart from this particular camera, the website also offers a very good range of gifts for all sports. Delivers mostly worldwide.

X-MI X-Minimax speakers
www.addonsworld.co.uk
The X-Minimax stereo system is perfect for music-loving travellers. It has two speakers and a built-in subwoofer, connected at the bottom by magnetic bases to form a capsule for easy storage. It weighs only 100g. Ships worldwide; express UK delivery.

Base layers, fleeces and jackets

www.blacks.co.uk

Adventurers' kit always carries a high price tag as it has to be the best. Make yourself popular and buy something at Blacks for your Adventurer, and if you're not sure what to choose, ask one of the shop staff. They are usually extremely knowledgeable (often being keen climbers, skiers, trekkers and campers themselves), but don't be persuaded to overspend. UK delivery.

Rucksack

www.cotswoldoutdoor.com

Apparently, rucksacks are extremely precious things that can't be shared. (Sholto, are you listening?) A good one of the right size is absolutely essential, so buy the best you can afford (having asked the intended recipient which one is wanted). Worldwide delivery.

Camelbak Cloudwalker

www.fieldandtrek.com

The Camelbak hydrating system gives constant, easy, hands-free access to hydration all the time, and is an essential part of any Adventurer's kit. The bag and stopper can be easily replaced if they get broken or lost. Worldwide delivery.

iPod waterproof case

www.ipodworld.co.uk

Since many Adventurers seem welded to their iPods and often get themselves wet (along with everything they're carrying), buy them an H20Audio waterproof case from somewhere like iPodWorld. Using this, and the waterproof headphones, they can listen to their iPods at depths of up to 3 metres with no ill effects. It comes with a sport armband as well. Worldwide express delivery.

Belgian adventurer Fons Oerlemans was famed for crossing the Atlantic Ocean on a truck attached to a home-made raft. In 2003 he began searching for a brewery to sponsor his latest adventure: a transatlantic crossing in a 6 tonne steel-framed bottle fitted with a motor, a kitchen and a bedroom.

> '*There are two kinds of adventurers: those who go truly hoping to find adventure and those who go secretly hoping they won't.*'
>
> WILLIAM TROGDON

Floating compass keyring

www.millets.co.uk

The Eurohike keyring compass has a floating needle in a liquid-filled plastic sphere and would make a perfect Adventurer's stocking filler, as would many of the other very reasonably priced products offered on this website, such as gloves, hats and hiking socks. Express UK delivery.

Leatherman tool

www.mindyourfingers. co.uk

The Leatherman is the multi-tool favoured by adventurers everywhere. You might have come across them already. They're certainly expensive, but they're the best and you'll

> '*You can't cross the sea merely by standing and staring at the water.*'
>
> RABINDRANATH TAGORE

never go wrong if you buy an Adventurer one of these. UK delivery; express available.

Compass watch

www.nomadtravel.co.uk

The Origo Watch Compass is a highly functional watch with a built-in compass and large, clear face: no longer will the recipient be able to make excuses about not knowing the time and getting lost. The face has 16 cardinal point segments and digital direction indication. Ships worldwide; express UK delivery.

Nanok sleeping bag

www.outdoorgb.com

You might think that this is a strange kind of gift, but having two trekkers/campers in my family, I know how important a really good sleeping bag is. If you're looking to buy for someone who's travelling soon, check up where they're going before you invest to make sure that what you buy is for the correct climate. Ships worldwide; express UK delivery.

Money card

www.postoffice.co.uk

Many far-off places take only-Visa, which is annoying if you or yours normally carry other types of card. You can get the Visa Travel Money Card from main post offices, load it with the amount you want, and top it up as necessary by making a phone call. It's a safe and secure way of carrying money.

When famed American adventurer Richard Halliburton announced his plan to swim the length of the Panama Canal in 1928, the authorities warned that they could operate the locks only for ships. Halliburton promptly dubbed himself the SS Halliburton and was allowed to swim through. Like all 'vessels', however, SS Halliburton had to pay a tonnage toll. Weighing 140 pounds, he paid 36 cents.

Pacsafe Travelsafe

www.roamingfox.co.uk

To avoid having to deal with that 'I've lost my passport/tickets/money, Mum' phone call, buy your Adventurer a lightweight and portable travel safe that can be locked and attached to a piece of furniture, such as a bed. Ships worldwide; express UK delivery.

Torches

www.thetorchshop.co.uk

I don't know what happens to the torches in my house, but they never, ever stay where they're supposed to. Really good torches make great gifts, and at the Torch Shop you can choose from Maglite, Cybalite, LED and wind-up torches, as well as the head-torch, essential for adventurers.

Travel health kit

www.travelpharm.co.uk

First aid and health kits aren't always at the top of the shopping list for a trip, but they're indispensible, so get the best you can find. The recipient might not thank you as much as you'd like before setting off, but the kit could well end up being the most appreciated gift ever received. UK delivery; express available.

BOOKWORM

*T*he bookworm usually combines a passion for books with a hobby, such as history, cooking or adventuring (see page 114). You'll know a bookworm by the state of their house. There are books everywhere – not tidily put away (the tidy ones are not proper bookworms; to qualify they must have at least a dozen books on the go at the same time), but scattered around the place – seven on the kitchen counter, four on the table by the sofa, three by the bed, with several left open or bookmarked. Forget anyone who has a smart pile of books in their loo for you to while away the time. They might think they're bookworms, but they're definitely just pretending – and I know these things!

In my family there's only one true bookworm. He has a special chair in the kitchen by the bookshelf so he can easily deliver books to the table. He leaves them all over the place, some opened and some closed. He never, ever puts them away, and if anyone else tries to, they're in trouble. Tidiness addicts who visit our house feel faint at the sight of all the clutter.

I'm not going to suggest which books to buy for people; all you need to do (as usual) is think about what your bookworm already likes to read and do. Then you can either find the latest volume to cover the subject, or buy something really special, such as a first edition or signed copy. Most people have a bit of the bookworm in them, and the list of stores that follows is a great place to start.

Abe Books
www.abebooks.co.uk
This is the worldwide marketplace for rare, second-hand and out of print books. You just need to search for the title or author of the book you're looking for. If available, a choice of editions will be shown immediately. You can then narrow your search to select first editions, signed copies and other options. Ships worldwide; express UK delivery.

Amazon
www.amazon.co.uk
There's not much I need to tell you about Amazon as you prob-

'There is a great deal of difference between an eager man who wants to read a book and a tired man who wants a book to read.'

G.K. CHESTERTON

ably use it for shopping already. This online store has a pretty comprehensive book range, and also sells just about everything else you might need. If you're buying for lots of bookworms, it's worth subscribing to the Amazon Prime feature: simply pay a basic price for postage, then first class mail is free in the UK, whatever you buy, and however many times you do so.

Blackwells of Oxford
www.blackwells.co.uk
What you'll find here is a really excellent and personal service, with a clear path through to the various departments: fiction, leisure and lifestyle, science, humanities, arts, medical, business, finance and law. There are some good discounts to be found, and shipping is free within the UK on orders over £20.

Book Depository
www.bookdepository.co.uk
The online Book Depository claims to be the fastest growing book distributor in Europe,

'I was a bookworm, and very skinny, with big, thick glasses. I never went on dates, and guys were afraid of me because I was smart. So I got contact lenses, started to dress a little better, and tried not to talk about Plato with boys. It worked!'

JULIANNE MOORE

and there's certainly a huge selection of books available via their easy-to-navigate website, which includes titles that can be printed to order. This is one of the best places to find books that have eluded you elsewhere. They offer free delivery to most countries worldwide.

Borders and Books Etc
www.borders.co.uk
www.booksetc.net
Books etc is owned by Borders, and the two chains have a similar philosophy. At both you'll find a great selection of books, and you can also sign up for their email bulletins, which mean you'll be the first to find out about in-store promotions, competitions and events near you. There is a useful function called a book suggester, and an invitation to join their new book group.

Foyles
www.foyles.co.uk
This is undoubtedly one of the world's most famous bookshops, where you'll find not only an extremely wide range of books, but also sheet music and manuscript paper, tickets for in-store author events, and a selection of signed copies. Ships worldwide; express UK delivery and gift wrapping.

Hatchards
www.hatchards.co.uk
Hatchards, founded in 1797, is the longest-established bookshop in London, and is now based in luxurious premises at 187 Piccadilly, next door to Fortnum & Mason. They have a very good choice of titles, including fiction, children's books, art and architecture, biography, food and wine, gardening, history and humour. They specialise in signed and

special editions. Ships world-wide; express UK delivery.

Jonkers Rare Books
www.jonkers.co.uk

Jonkers specialise in modern first editions, fine illustrated books, classic children's fiction and 19th-century literature. So if you have a godchild who might appreciate a first edition of Michael Bond's *Paddington Goes to Town* or works by A.A. Milne, Enid Blyton, Lewis Carroll and many more, you'll find it here. Call to order; world-wide delivery.

Little Bookworms
www.littlebookworms.co.uk

Little Bookworms is a family business offering books, software and activity packs for ages 0–11. The website is divided into sections so that you can choose by age and then by type of book, theme or author. It's really quick to use, and every book includes a detailed review. UK delivery and gift wrapping.

Redhouse
www.redhouse.co.uk

Red House specialises in children's books for all ages, from babies to young adults. They produce a catalogue each month, featuring an introduction from a leading author, and their bright and colourful website carries a wide selection of hand-picked books that is updated regularly. UK delivery and gift wrapping.

Waterstones
www.waterstones.co.uk

Waterstone's website is very easy to use and refreshingly uncluttered. You can browse categories, such as business, finance and law, computing, education, comics and graphic novels, as well as the more usual fiction, children's books, cookery and sport. Delivery is free on orders over £15 within the UK. Surface or courier services for international orders.

W H Smith
www.whsmith.co.uk

This easy-on-the-eye website offers books (often at very good discounts), all the latest DVDs, music and computer games, plus a small selection from the stationery ranges. You will find a wide variety of gift ideas, including commemorative sports books and facsimiles of historic newspapers. You can also subscribe at a discount to all your favourite magazines. UK delivery.

BOY RACER

*T*he Boy Racer is a very special species. Almost always over forty, and most likely over fifty, he's in love with his cars. You will be able to spot one at Silverstone or Goodwood from time to time, but he generally prefers to be doing the driving himself in whatever souped-up vehicle he's been able to lay his hands on. Not for him the latest Audi or Merc. Cars are not rated simply in terms of looks and value; what's going on under the bonnet is infinitely more important. The Boy Racer may never be able to reach top speed in his precious motor – he'll never find the right road – but he'll do pretty well, quite often encouraged by a young son, who sits in the front passenger seat, while the child's mother cowers in the back. In my case (I'm married to a Boy Racer) I sometimes refuse to travel in the same car at all.

In this section's listings I've included the makes of satellite navigation system and camera detector that we use in our household. There are, of course, many others, and you should always compare before buying to make sure you're getting the best deal. Amazon frequently offers the most competitive price.

'Here comes 40. I'm feeling my age and I've ordered the Ferrari. I'm going to get the whole mid-life crisis package.'

KEANU REEVES

Motor-racing books
www.amazon.co.uk

There are some excellent books about motor racing. Here are just a few suggestions from the current crop in the shops: *Winning Is Not Enough* by Jackie Stewart (Headline); *Motor Racing: Extraordinary Images from 1900 to 1970* by John Tennant (Cassell) and *The Official Formula 1 Season Review* (Haynes). Ships worldwide; express UK delivery plus gift wrapping.

Men's driving gloves
www.dunhill.com

Dunhill surely make some of the most beautiful driving gloves ever. Available in soft nappa leather in several colours, they're exceptionally luxurious and yes, frighteningly expensive, but they would be a wonderful gift. If you don't want to fork out quite so much, visit www.aspinaloflondon. com for some other options of superb quality. Ships worldwide; express UK delivery and gift wrapping.

Grand Prix tickets
www.formula1.com
www.grandprix-tickets.com

OK, it's a luxury gift, but if you can, why not? I know several Boy Racers who are regularly off to Brands Hatch, Monaco and other Grand Prix destinations. There are several websites where you can book your tickets, but I've chosen these two for being easy to browse and informative. At www.formula1.com you are directed through Expedia, so you can book your flights, hotels and race tickets as a package. With www.grandprix-tickets.com you need to make your own travel arrangements.

Goodwood Festival of Speed
www.goodwood.co.uk

The first Festival of Speed was held in June 1993, when the Earl of March brought motor sport back to Goodwood. Tickets must be bought in advance – and sell out fast – so register your interest on the website. For those who enjoy a more retro feel, the annual Goodwood Revival in the autumn is a spectacular and memorable event. (Make sure you have flat shoes, girls, as you'll definitely need them.) If you give Goodwood tickets as a gift, make sure you pre-book a table at one of the restaurants. The website features some wonderful classic gifts too.

The Italian Job (1969)

www.play.com

Every Boy Racer should have a copy of this film, starring Michael Caine, Noel Coward and Benny Hill. Forget the remake (although I did enjoy it, and it's worth buying with the original as a set). This is a cult 1960s' movie and contains one of the craziest car chases in cinema history. It's simply an essential buy.

Speed camera detector

www.roadangel.co.uk

Essential for all those with a tendency to drive a bit too fast, a speed camera detector can definitely help them to retain their licence. As someone who has been caught when driving over 30 mph a couple of times, I can say with feeling that a detector does make you think constantly about how fast you're going. This is an essential piece of kit.

Silverstone Driving Experience

www.silverstone.co.uk

The Boy Racers in your life may well tell you that they can drive fast in their own car, but when do they get the chance? Give them a day out, or even part of a day out, driving on the Silverstone circuit and they'll have a great time. Make sure you're involved in the booking as well as the giving to be certain that your gift is used before it expires.

Snooper Strabo sat nav

www.snooperdirect.com

If the Boy Racer in your life doesn't already have one, the latest satellite navigation system with built-in speed camera detector is a wonderful gift. It's also appropriate for any new drivers in your family who have recently passed their driving test and are still in that honeymoon period of wanting to drive everyone everywhere. (It doesn't last, so make the most of it!) UK delivery with express option.

Aston Martin keyring

www.extremeautoaccessories.co.uk

Really silly, but a great stocking filler. Apart from the Aston Martin, there are lots of other keyrings here, from Ford Capris to 4 x 4 Jeeps. Take care, though – men are touchy about their cars, so don't give one of these if he's easily offended! UK and Ireland delivery.

Denbigh Boy Racer

I'm a Denbigh boy racer on a daredevil drive,
Dodging all the traffic on the A55,
Light on the steering wheel, heavy on the gas,
Cutting out the corners in the Nant-y-Garth Pass.

Screaming up Vale Street scaring old biddies,
Circling the car park practising my skiddies,
Rocket-ship engine revving up the NOS,
Blacked-out windows, Hugo Boss.

Bright blue neons lit up underneath,
Fender on the front like a pair of false teeth,
Rear wing, big bore, spoiler at the back,
Turning our estate into a racing track.

I'm a Denbigh boy racer on the Denbigh Moors,
Wheels like ice skates, flame-thrower doors,
Hurtling about with a gang of hot chicks,
I'm a Denbigh boy racer...and I'm eighty-six!

GARETH GLYN ROBERTS

The Little Book of Fast Cars

www.bookrabbit.com

This compilation by Philip Raby features some of the fastest road cars ever to have been built. It includes a short biography and performance figures for each model, and is packed with wonderful photographs. Book Rabbit offers an ever-changing choice of titles about cars. UK delivery.

Subscription to *Top Gear* magazine

www.topgear.com

Most Boy Racers will have collected all the books and DVDs, by Jeremy Clarkson and his co-presenters, so why not give a subscription to *Top Gear* magazine instead? The only problem? You'll never hear the end of what his next car will be, let alone how he's going to afford it. Worldwide delivery.

CULTURE
VULTURE

*T*his section is dedicated to the type of person who, when you're on a perfectly normal shopping trip to Paris, Milan or New York, will frantically turn the pages of their guidebook to find the nearest museum/art gallery/notable building and pay visits lasting at least half a day. You might realise that this description doesn't apply to me. Anything operatic or music-orientated and I'm likely to be interested, but I generally stay well clear of walking slowly through museum or galleries for hours on end, no matter how stunning the displays.

So what do you buy for the art-loving culture vulture? A pair of comfortable shoes, perhaps? Er, maybe not. You'd be better off finding out what kind of art they love and where they like to find it, then working out what you can afford. That original van Gogh may be just a little outside your budget, but there are many affordable alternatives.

An obvious choice for the art lover would be to buy a book on their favoured topic, so visit your local bookshop, or go online to the major booksellers (see page 118) and check what's available there. New editions, preferably in hardback, with beautiful reproductions of fine art, make very good gifts. Also look at some of the other ideas given in this section for both art and music lovers.

ART
Art Institute of Chicago

www.artinstituteshop.org

The online shop contains a sumptuous range of items from around the world that you almost certainly won't find elsewhere. It includes wonderful books and scrolls, sculptures, throws, coasters and mugs. Worldwide shipping.

MoMA

www.momastore.org

The poster and print section at the Museum of Moden Art in New York is wide and varied. You will find reproductions of works by Chagall, Dali, Van Gogh and Frank Lloyd Wright, plus dozens of others, which you can order as posters, billboards or framed and matted prints. Worldwide shipping to most destinations.

National Portrait Gallery

www.npg.org.uk

Pay a visit to the NPG online shop and you can take out a subscription to the gallery for a friend. Alternatively, choose from their selection of high-quality, side-tied notebooks, art books, prints, mugs and other gifts. Worldwide delivery.

Royal Academy

www.royalacademy.org.uk

Treat someone special to a year's membership of the Royal Academy in its beautiful buildings near the elegant Burlington Arcade just off Piccadilly in London. (The members' room boasts some of the comfiest sofas in central London.) You can also buy individual tickets to the fabulous exhibitions held at the RA, or pay a visit to the online shop, where you'll find cards, limited edition prints, diaries and calendars, plus a range of other lovely gifts. Will deliver worldwide.

Telescope Planet

www.telescopeplanet.co.uk

Here you'll find a really good range of opera glasses and mini-telescopes for lovers of the arts, with prices from the extremely reasonable to the

'I'm a culture vulture, and I just want to experience it all.'

DEBBIE HARRY

very expensive. You can also find birdwatcher binoculars, brass admiral zoom telescopes, laser pointers and reusable hand-warmers (the last being essential for touring architectural wonders in cold climates). UK delivery; express available.

The Tate
www.tate.org.uk
The Tate is a collection of four UK galleries that includes Tate Modern, Tate Britain, Tate Liverpool and Tate St Ives. The gift shops and website offer an excellent (and clever) selection of gifts, ranging from membership and tours to art materials, prints and posters, cards and art-led designer accessories.

The Wallace Collection
www.wallacecollection.org
Admission to the Wallace Collection is free of charge, so why not take someone on a surprise visit and then buy them lunch or dinner at the Wallace Restaurant, one of the most highly acclaimed restaurants to be found in an art gallery? Alternatively, if you can't get there in person, visit the online shop, where there's an excellent collection of art books and guides, stationery and cards.

MUSIC AND THEATRE
Glyndebourne
www.glyndebourne.com
Glyndebourne in East Sussex is my favourite place in the UK for opera, and the online shop is a treasure trove of unusual finds. Some are Glyndebourne associated, such as the pretty mugs they produce each year; others, such as the beautiful silver pieces by Pruden & Smith, are simply included on

John Christie and his wife Audrey Mildmay had a dream and a passion. They wanted to provide a quality venue for opera lovers. On 28 May 1834 the curtain rose on the first opera festival at their estate at Glyndebourne. Christie said it was 'not the best we can do, but the best that can be done anywhere'.

merit. Are you looking for a special present for a new baby who happens to have opera-loving parents? Put his or her name on the membership list. It might take a good few years before the little mite is willing or able to join, but it will be well worth the wait.

The O2 Arena
www.the02.co.uk
This dramatic building, located on the river at Greenwich in southeast London, hosts a wealth of shows and events. If you're thinking of giving tickets or a night out as a gift, have a look at the variety on offer. From spectacular entertainments such as Cirque du Soleil, to song and dance shows and rock concerts, there's a tremendous amount to choose from. Find out what your culture vulture likes, then go book.

The Royal Opera House
www.royalopera.org
There has been a theatre on the ROH site in Covent Garden since 1728, but the present building was opened in 1999. It is home to the Royal Ballet as well as opera, and is a wonderful place to find gifts for the opera lover in your life. The website is beautifully designed, and if you want to book seats online, you can see and choose exactly where they will be. There are high-quality opera glasses and well-priced 'orchestral mugs' amongst the gifts in the ROH shop.

ARTS IN PRINT
History of the Theatre
www.amazon.co.uk
This comprehensive survey of theatre history by Oscar Brockett and Franklin Hildy has been a classic for more than thirty years. It includes over 500 photos and illustrations, and the expertise of one of the most respected historians in the field. Every theatre lover should have a copy. Ships worldwide; express UK delivery plus gift wrapping.

Magazines
www.magazine-group.co.uk
With over 400 titles on offer, and some very good discounts, you could find a magazine subscription for just about anyone here, from the art addict (*Apollo*), music fanatic (*The Gramophone*), food and wine lover (*Decanter*) to the interiors enthusiast (*Beautiful Homes*) and fashion fiend (*Vogue*).

DANCING QUEEN

*T*he Dancing Queen is of the female sex, and usually aged between 12 and 25, although she sometimes remains in this category for longer (which should be discouraged if she doesn't retain the svelte figure necessary for this look). She loves to wear tight jeans, high heels and layers of little tops, some of which have occasionally been known to cover her midriff. Her jeans are often decorated with the biggest sparkly belt she can lay her hands on. Dancing Queens travel in packs, to the point where they seem unable to do anything on their own. If this sounds like someone you know, take heart – they are incredibly easy to buy for.

Music

www.amazon.co.uk
www.hmv.com
www.play.com

There are so many great on and offline music stores that it's impossible to list them all, so here are a few. Make absolutely sure before you splash out that you know what your Dancing Queen likes listening to. Don't even try to guess as you'll almost certainly get

it wrong. Ask her siblings if you're not sure, *not* her parents – they won't have a clue.

Anything iPod

www.apple.com

If you're being nagged at for the new generation Nano or iPod, take a look here first to check on the latest colours and products. Then you can have a look around (oh no, not again) at www.amazon.co.uk, www.

johnlewis.com and price comparison website www.kelkoo.co.uk to make sure you're getting the best deal. Delivery depends on which store you use.

Calvin Klein lingerie
www.figleaves.com
Yes, you have to know your recipient really quite well to go down this route, but nothing – and I mean *nothing* – I have bought for my daughter by Calvin Klein has been a disappointment, whereas many other brands have. It's definitely a cult collection and you will be popular if you buy from here. Ships worldwide; express UK delivery and gift wrapping.

iPod Travel Speakers
www.goplanetgo.co.uk
Yes, I know, iPod again, but how can you go wrong? Having bought these speakers for two of my kids, I thought you should know about them as they're really small and make quite a good sound. They're also available in colours to match the iPod. Don't forget the headphones, or you'll have to listen to the DQ's music as well. Ships worldwide; express UK delivery.

La Senza knickers or PJs
www.lasenza.co.uk
My daughter tells me that this is the place she wants her essentials to come from, particularly cute-slogan pyjamas and perfect undies. Well, she should know. You can either pick something yourself, provided you're sure of her size, or give her a gift voucher – not quite so much fun to unwrap, but more fun to use. Ships worldwide; express UK delivery and gift wrapping.

Dangly earrings
www.mikeyjewellery.com
Mikey is great for sparkly, dangly and over the top jewels that won't break the bank. You can find their designs in lots of department stores, or browse their range online and let yourself be guided by them to the latest 'must-have' creation.

'You are the dancing queen, young and sweet, only seventeen...'

'DANCING QUEEN', ABBA

> '*My mother told me I was dancing before I was born. She could feel my toes tapping wildly inside her for months.*'
>
> GINGER ROGERS

Expect to pay between £15 and £50. At the time of writing delivery was free.

Mamma Mia DVD
www.play.com

Every Dancing Queen is going to want a copy of this movie, if they don't have it already (so find out first). Any wet blanket who says it's too silly/Pierce Brosnan can't sing/I don't like the music obviously hasn't seen it. It's a wonderful, feel-good film, and one to be treasured and brought out whenever a bit of stress-busting is needed. Ships worldwide; gift wrapping available.

Pretty ballet flats
www.prettyballerinas.com

These are an essential part of every Dancing Queen's wardrobe – when she can't walk any

> '*I could have danced all night...*'
>
> WORDS SUNG BY ELIZA DOOLITTLE IN *MY FAIR LADY*

further in her silly heels she'll need something flat, comfortable, chic and danceable-in to bring out of her handbag. Do I hear some say 'Ballet pumps are going out of fashion'? How silly is that? They'll always be essential. Worldwide delivery.

Music posters
www.pushposters.com

Pushposters almost certainly offers the largest range of music posters in the world, featuring over 1500 different artists from all genres of music, ranging from the smallest independent bands right up to best-selling stadium acts. They also have related T-shirts, hoodies, caps and hats, calendars, keyrings, wallets, bags and other accessories. Worldwide delivery.

'Of the moment' jeans
www.riverisland.com
www.topshop.com

River Island and Top Shop are the destinations of choice for the Dancing Queen in my family, although if she could get me to fork out, we'd be going somewhere pricier in a flash. I'm not going to suggest that you buy skinny, boot-cut, high-rise or any other type of jeans here, as whatever I suggest now might well have changed by the time this book comes out. If you prefer, you can get a cute little cardi. (Dancing Queens don't wear pashminas, unless they're pinching one of yours because it matches their dress.) River Island always has a good selection Express UK delivery (both stores) and gift wrapping (Top Shop).

Sparkly belt
www.rodeobelts.co.uk
Here you can find the perfect belt for anyone who likes to dress up their jeans with heels and something gorgeous, glittery and quite over the top around their waist. If that's you

> 'Sure [Fred Astaire] was great, but don't forget Ginger Rogers did everything he did backwards...and in high heels!'
>
> BOB THAVES

or someone you know, you'll feel totally at home on this website. The belts and buckles are decorated with the highest-quality crystals and ornamental stones, and there's a very good range of colours and hides to choose from. Worldwide delivery and gift wrapping.

Concert tickets
www.ticketmaster.co.uk
My son recently bought his sister six tickets so that she and five friends could go to hear one of her favourite bands – a gift rapturously received. (He even ferried the group there and back – a big deal as he was no fan of the band itself.) If you want to do something similar, make sure you know the bands she likes.

Top Shop Gift Card
www.topshop.com
This is a great gift for any girl: you can put as much on it as you want and top it up from time to time, should you feel so inclined. They can then go out and buy things with it that you think are totally unsuitable. If you give one to your favourite goddaughter, be ready to duck when her mother comes to call. Ships worldwide; express UK delivery and gift wrapping.

FASHION VICTIM

*B*e extremely careful when buying for 'fashion victims', and don't buy unless you're absolutely sure you can cope with the stress, misery and injustice of getting it even the tiniest, teeniest bit wrong. If you do get it wrong, you'll not only be looked down upon from a great height, but you will also lose any standing you ever had with these totally uncompromising individuals. They know exactly what they should be wearing, carrying or tottering around on.

The female of the species reads *Daily Candy* and *Fashion Confidential* every day, even if she doesn't have the time, to ensure that she never falls out of vogue. She's clever too. If snakeskin is 'in', you'll never see her wearing it from top to toe; she'll sport a tiny piece, a hint, a soupçon – a narrow belt, a trim on a bag, or a slim cuff. If 'stars' are the fad, they'll probably be dangling from her ears, not plastered all over her cardigan (should she wear such a thing), and if platforms have made a comeback, you can bet your life she'll be tottering along with the best: they'll be peeping out from under her 7 For All Mankind jeans, which will fit her perfectly and be in the latest rinse. They may be skinny, bootcut, boyfriend, highrise or whatever cut came into fashion a split second ago.

Anna

www.shopatanna.co.uk

With stores in London, Norfolk and Suffolk, Anna is an innovative boutique offering clothes and accessories by Betty Jackson, Seven, Issa London, Orla Kiely, Gharani Strock and lesser known designers, such as Day and Noa Noa. Ships worldwide; express UK delivery and gift wrapping.

ASOS

www.asos.com

Click through the sections on this site to find All Saints, French Connection, Just Cavalli and Rock & Republic alongside bags by Balenciaga, watches by Michael Kors and footwear by Kurt Geiger, Strutt Couture and Ugg. Ships worldwide; express UK delivery.

Brittique

www.brittique.com

This is a beautifully designed online boutique featuring designers such as Amanda Wakeley, Maria Grachvogel and Louise Amstrap, and their list is growing all the time. You'll find accessories and jewellery by Vinnie Day, Lucy J, Deal & Wire and more, some of which would make perfect gifts. Worldwide delivery.

Browns

www.brownsfashion.com

The Browns website offers a mouthwatering assortment of contemporary designers, including Lanvin, Balenciaga, Missoni and Paul Smith, as well as Dolce & Gabbana, Roberto Cavalli, Ann Demeulemeester and Issa. For gifts, take a look first at the accessories section. Ships worldwide; express UK delivery and gift wrapping.

Bunny Hug

www.bunnyhug.co.uk

Bunny Hug offers each season's fashion and celebrity 'must-haves' from around the globe, with a broad mix of items ranging from well-priced fashion pieces right through to luxury items. If you've seen it out there but can't find it on this website, you can email them and they'll tell you if a) they already have it on order or b) they can find it for you – and you can't ask for more than that, can you? Ships worldwide; express UK delivery.

Coggles

www.coggles.com

There's a really good range of modern brands at this online boutique, including Joesph, 7 For All Mankind, Nicole Farhi,

Paul Smith and Ralph Lauren. You can select by brand or type of product, and the pictures are extremely clear. Ships worldwide; express UK delivery.

Croc & Co
www.crocandco.co.uk

This is an excellent multi-brand designer boutique offering collections by Issa, Hudson, Paul Smith, Vivienne Westwood, Valentino, Nicole Farhi and more, and the range changes regularly. Unlike some online boutiques, this one doesn't try to overwhelm you with products: on one page you can select by designer, by men, women or children's clothes and by type of garment. Buy your little darling's next Issa dress from here. Ships worldwide; express UK delivery.

Cruise Clothing
www.cruiseclothing.co.uk

Cruise offers an excellent range of contemporary fashion for men and women, specialising in casual wear, trainers, bags and shoes. With brands such as Gina, Chloe, Marc Jacobs, Dior and DKNY, there's plenty to choose from and lots of ideas for gifts, if you can bear to give them away. Standard UK delivery is free.

Joseph M
www.josephm.com

This women's and children's designer boutique based in Darlington offers ranges by Ralph Lauren, See by Chloe, Issa, Alexander McQueen, James Lakeland and Matthew Williamson. In 'What's Hot" you can see the latest trends for all ages. Ships worldwide; express UK delivery.

Jules B
www.julesb.co.uk

Brands here include Armani Jeans, Nicole Farhi, Diane von Furstenberg, Mulberry, Oska, Crea Concept and Hoss Intropia. The next time you find that the better-known stores have sold out of the designer piece you're looking for, take a look here – you might just find it. Ships worldwide; express UK delivery and gift wrapping.

Matches
www.matchesfashion.com

This luxury designer boutique is famous for offering a unique

'If Botticelli was alive today, he'd be working for Vogue.'

PETER USTINOV

personal service together with an enticing choice of designers, such as Dolce & Gabbana, Bottega Veneta, Chloe, Christian Louboutin, Lanvin, Marc Jacobs, Missoni and Stella McCartney. Ships worldwide; express UK delivery and gift wrapping.

My Theresa
www.mytheresa.com
Be sure to click on the English version here, unless your German is exceptionally good, as this online boutique is based in Munich. The talent list here is exceptional, with designers such as Anna Sui, Catherine Malandrino, Dolce & Gabbana, Christian Louboutin, Vera Wang, Temperley and Miu Miu being just a small example. Ships worldwide; gift wrapping available.

My Wardrobe
www.my-wardrobe.com
This designer clothing and accessories website is very well laid out – a refreshing change from some designer sites. Among the labels it sells are FrostFrench, Ann Louise Roswald, Sara Berman, Tocca and See by Chloe. Ships worldwide; express UK delivery.

Net-a-Porter
www.netaporter.com
This site is known worldwide as one of the best for fashion. If you're after a reasonably priced gift, take a look at their excellent collections of contemporary jewellery. Whatever's on the current 'hot list', you'll find it here. Worldwide express and gift wrapping available.

Reiss
www.reiss.co.uk
You've seen the label in the stores – now you can buy this fast-expanding, contemporary, reasonably priced and 'fashion forward' brand online. Choose from up-to-the-minute outerwear, dresses, tailoring and casual separates, plus excellent chic accessories. UK and Ireland delivery.

Start
www.start-london.com
Where 'Fashion meets Rock 'n' roll' is the mission statement here, and you'll immediately see why – Marc Jacobs and Mulberry mix happily with Josh Goot and Pink Soda. There are clothes and accessories for both men and women. Ships worldwide; express UK delivery.

FILM BUFF

*F*ilm Buffs are totally different from Book-worms, and not just because they're interested in totally different media. The Bookworm reads and enjoys lots of books, but doesn't need to show off about them; the Film Buff, on the other hand, loves to show off, and isn't happy unless telling you about all the films he or she has seen, on HD, DVD or in the cinema.

Films are probably only one of enthusiasms of your particular buff because people addicted to cinema are often keen on music and computer games too, so I've included listings for these things as well (in fact, many of the sites sell films, CDs *and* games). However, if you know your Film Buff and his collection well, you're pretty safe in buying a film to plug a particular gap. Listen out for the person's likes or dislikes., and don't buy, for example, *Dirty Dancing* for someone who's more of a *Midnight Cowboy* fan. Your gift will simply be passed on or pushed to the back of a cupboard. One of the best gifts is a clever/funny/original boxed set containing an actor or genre you know the recipient is keen on.

A word of warning: don't, if you can possibly avoid it, let a Film Buff buy *you* a movie because it'll probably be something obscure and subtitled.

Movies – and Games and Music

There are, as I'm sure you know, a huge number of online places where you can buy movies. together with music and games, gadgets, games consoles, books and all the other products that these websites are branching into. As there are far too many to list, I've given you just my favourite tried and tested retailers, but you might well know more.

There's no doubt that as a customer you are in a win-win situation in this area. There is so much competition out there and they are all competing for your business. Make sure you take advantage of this and use one of the price comparison websites listed overleaf to ensure you get the best deal. As most of the retailers offer free delivery, you can cherry-pick who you buy from. Bear in mind that it will probably take longer to deliver from a website based in the Channel Islands, but these sites frequently offer the best prices, so take a bit of time and browse early.

> 'I like a film to have a beginning, a middle and an end, but not necessarily in that order.'
> JEAN LUC GODARD

Buff: a devotee or well-informed student of some activity or subject.

PRICE COMPARE HERE

If you're looking for a gift for a film buff and you don't price compare, you're really going to miss out, not to mention overspend. Get into the habit of using the following sites, always check on delivery costs (which are frequently free) and order at the best price you're offered: you'll save amazing amounts of money.

Best CD Price

www.best-cd-price.co.uk

Know the CD you'd like to buy, but want to make sure you get the best price? Use this price comparison website, which not only shows where you'll find the best deal, but includes the postage details as well, so you know just where you are.

DVD Price Check

www.dvdpricecheck.co.uk

If you're looking for a DVD, this is the place to start, as you can see what's available around the world and at what price. With so many possible places to spend you money, it's hard to know which option to choose. This site is a great help, and can save you hours of searching.

GamesTracker

www.uk.gamestracker.com

Your younger Film Buff is probably disguised as a Game Boy, and has similar traits. However much you might dislike those extremely noisy (and often violent) computer games, you won't want your kids spending more of their not-so-hard-earned pocket money than they need to, let alone you spending yours if you're buying a gift. This is the place to find out who's offering what and where.

BUY HERE
CD WOW

www.cdwow.com

Wow is right – this is a hugely busy and extremely successful online retailer, where you can buy CDs and DVDs as well as computer games and mobile phones. See also WOW rentals, with free trials and offers, WOW gifts, gadgets and

'You have Van Gogh's ear for music.'

BILLY WILDER

vouchers, and WOW Woman too. They offer free delivery worldwide for all items, and regular special offers.

Game

www.game.co.uk

Whatever the very latest games console is, you'll find it here, along with a wide selection of games and some very good prices. So consider buying here for the gamesmen in your family. Ships worldwide; express UK delivery.

HMV

www.hmv.co.uk

The HMV shops on Oxford Street and within Selfridges are usually the first places that my kids want to hit on a trip to London, and I quite understand why: whether you're looking for chart CDs or DVDs or something a bit more obscure, they're bound to have it. MP3 players together with film and music T-shirts and posters can be found here as well. Ships worldwide; express UK delivery.

Play

www.play.com

Music, movies, games and books at very good prices, with delivery included, are available

from this website, based in the Channel Islands. They offer a huge range of films on DVD, CDs and games for all systems, and special multi-buy offers at cheap prices – 30 per cent off specific boxed sets, and 40 per cent off a wide choice of current releases. Free worldwide delivery.

Sendit

www.sendit.com

At online store Sendit you'll find all the DVDs, games, CDs and small electronic gadgets you could possibly want (including the ever-popular iPod). When you buy you'll be joining their loyalty scheme and collecting iPoints automatically. Give them a try: they're definitely trying hard.

Zavvi

www.zavvi.co.uk

On this easy-to-use Guernsey-based website you can order all the latest releases, as well as pre-ordering the next 'must-have' CDs, DVDs and games. They don't always give you the full and discounted price information, and they may not always be the cheapest, but if you compare prices, you'll find they're not at the top end either. Free UK delivery.

GADGET CRAZY

*T*he true Gadgetman does not like ordinary, stupid gadgets-for-the-sake-of-them. He's an extremely talented individual and can make just about anything work, whether it's your new TV, sat nav, laptop or music system. He likes to be totally in control and will be extremely impatient if you don't immediately understand when he's trying to explain how something works (*he* doesn't understand why you don't already know). If you have someone like this in your household, you're extremely fortunate because not only can he make everything work, he can fix things too.

You have to be extremely careful when choosing a gift for Gadgetman as it needs to be cunning and clever, or he'll look at you as if you're totally stupid. Watch out too when a Gadgetman buys something for you, as you might well need maths A-level to use it. (My son, Sholto, falls in this category: 'Come and fix this for me, will you?')

Browse through the sites listed here, and also take a look at some of the gadget and gift shops listed in Father's Day, Adventurer and Happy Snapper (see pages 56, 114 and 148).

> Easily confused by technology? Contact the retailers direct and ask them for help. Most have general information on their websites, but will be happy to make specific recommendations if you ring.

8-in-1 Remote Control
www.firebox.com

From silly gadgets, chilli pea-nuts and scorpion vodka to high-tech toys your gadget fan will actually keep and use, such as digital photo frames, sleek 8-in-1 remote controls and The Bevy, an all-in-one iPod shuffle, keyring and bot-tle opener, you can find eve-rything here at a wide range of prices. Ships worldwide; ex-press UK delivery.

Portable espresso machine
www.iwantoneofthose.co.uk

An irresistible (and very clev-erly designed) gift and gadget shop with a huge choice and very accessible website. You can search by price or prod-uct type in various categories, from gadgets for the garden, kitchen and office to the inevi-table toys and games. Surely you know someone who'd love a portable espresso machine or a beatbox beanie hat? Ships worldwide; express UK deliv-ery and gift wrapping.

Slim G4 optical mouse
www.kjglobal.co.uk

There are some superb 'techie' gadgets here, many of which you won't find anywhere else. The company specialises in innovative products that have been developed abroad and buys direct from the manufac-turers. From security for your laptop to the NaviNote padless tablet pen there's a wonderful range of gifts for the gadget addict. Express worldwide de-livery.

Micro Zoomer 3D RC helicopter
www.paramountzone.com

There's an extensive selection of gadgets, games, boy's toys, bar items, mp3 players and lifestyle accessories on this website. Use the online gift finder for ideas on what to buy the 'gadget geek' in your life. Same-day dispatch for most UK orders; and they're happy to deliver worldwide.

VAIO TZ Series
www.sonystyle.co.uk

Here you can find all those gorgeously slim, small, modern laptops with VAIO on the front, which come in red, indigo, blue, gold and luxury pink (plus black, of course). They also sell the latest mega, mega pixel digital cameras, micro hifi and headphones. UK de-livery and express service.

GARDENING GURU

I'm not a gardener. Anyone who knows me (and they don't have to know me very well) can easily recognise this fact. Even when it comes to recognising the plants and trees in my garden, I am completely useless. Unfortunately, I appear to have passed on this trait to my children, who are occasionally willing to sit on the ride-on mower to cut the grass, but are totally uninterested in doing anything else horticultural. That said, I am nonetheless highly qualified to offer you advice on gifts for the gardening guru in your life as I have had several in my family. Steer away from the larger tools unless you know for certain that's what they want; and don't go near mowers, trimmers and chainsaws as those are far better left to the experts.

String in a tin

www.baileys-home-garden.co.uk

Baileys offer a wonderfully eclectic mix of home and garden accessories, from pretty Welsh blankets and paint buckets to big sinks, garden lighting, bubble bath and Carrot Hand Cream. They also have gift ideas for your junior gardener, such as tools and colourful watering cans, plus vintage-style garden forks, pots and twine reels. UK delivery.

Gardman oriental bird table

www.birstall.co.uk

All gardeners love to attract different varieties of bird to their garden, and this site has a very good selection of bird tables, ranging from a reasonably priced oriental table made of resin to beautiful hand-crafted items in wood. Birstall's also sells birdseed, and just about everything else the gardening enthusiast might need. Worldwide delivery.

Gothic-style bird table

www.crocus.co.uk

Crocus is one of the best websites for gardeners. It not only offers attractive flowers and plants, giving you more information about them than most, but also supplies just about everything else you might need for the garden, all presented in a really attractive and informative way. UK delivery; express available.

Suede gardening gauntlets

www.franceshilary.com

Here's a wonderful place to find gifts for the gardener in your life. The products combine practicality with style, and most would make excellent presents. There are beautifully made classic tools, such as dibbers and tampers, gloves and aprons, wonderful boots, and carefully thought-out gift sets. Ships worldwide; express UK delivery and gift wrapping.

Chinese blue wicker trug

www.gardentrading.co.uk

There's a very wide range of prices here, as Garden Trading offers everything from unusual pieces of furniture, such as the Broomstick Bench, to interesting canisters and glassware, and the Lisa Stickley collection of cushions, enamel mugs and matchbox covers. UK delivery.

Kew Gardens footed bowl

www.thecountrygardener. co.uk

Calling itself 'the online emporium for country gardeners', this site offers an exceptional choice of tools and accessories, ranging from plant ties and net tunnels to potting benches and planters. This glazed bowl I've selected is perfect for filling with forced narcissi or hyacinths for an indoor winter display. UK delivery.

Grab-o-saurus lifting device

www.giftsforgardeners.co.uk

This futuristic lifting device is robust, lightweight and designed to work on any surface. It simplifies many chores that result in a bent back, but don't be tempted to give it to someone you don't know quite well as they might think you're being cheeky about their age or agility; however, it would make a great gift for an older gardener or anyone with back problems. Worldwide delivery.

Blackcurrant bush

www.glut.co.uk

Glut offers a wide selection of well-photographed gifts – all beautifully packaged and hand-tied with raffia – for any of your friends who like to garden and eat/drink as well. You'll find

'The best way to garden is to put on a wide-brimmed straw hat and some old clothes. And with a hoe in one hand and a cold drink in the other, tell somebody else where to dig.'

TEXAS BIX BENDER

sloe gin accompanying young sloe trees, a bottle of Macon with a white grape vine, and champagne with terracotta pots planted with sage, thyme, oregano and rosemary. UK delivery; express service and gift wrapping available.

Zinc lantern set

www.grandillusions.co.uk

Here you can choose from ranges of reasonably priced accessories, including storm lanterns, candelabra, votive glasses, French scented candles and guest soaps. There's also a wide selection of small, pretty items for outdoors, such as traditional watering cans, bird feeders, sconces and glass carriers. UK delivery.

Iron bootjack and brushes

www.plantstuff.com

The Plant Stuff website is beautifully laid out, and here you can buy braziers and hammocks, candles in metal pots, slate cheeseboards, lead ducks and Hunter clogs and wellies. They also offer a wonderful gardener's hamper, although most gardeners would almost certainly have some of the items included already. Returns are free. EU delivery.

RHS membership
www.rhs.org.uk

The Royal Horticultural Society is based at Wisley in Surrey. You can enrol someone as a member via their website, and the deal includes a monthly magazine, reduced tickets to RHS flower shows, and free entry into RHS and partner gardens. You can also search for gifts via RHS Shopping Online, which will invite you to the Wisley Bookshop and their other online shopping areas. Worldwide delivery.

Leather-handled topiary shears
www.rkalliston.com

This is a really exceptional retailer offering perfect gifts for the gardener, from wasp catchers and storm lanterns to twine and dibbers, hammocks (to rest in after a hard day) and fairy vases, as well as gardeners' gift sets, china for alfresco dining, and pretty flower baskets. Ships worldwide; express UK delivery.

Baby olive tree
www.treesdirect.co.uk

Fruit and nut trees, ornamentals, and aromatic, evergreen bays are just some of the unusual gift ideas you can find here. The trees are chosen for their colour, blossom, shape and size to suit all types of gardens. They arrive in a sack tied with green garden string, together with planting instructions and a handwritten message card. EU delivery; express option available.

Burgon & Ball indoor watering can
www.wyevale.co.uk

Most gardeners love to grow things inside, and have to admit that the usual green plastic watering can doesn't add much to the decor. The Burgon & Ball design I'm suggesting is both pretty and functional, and comes from a garden supplies retailer that offers just about everything the gardening guru could possibly need. UK mainland delivery.

'Our England is a garden,
and such gardens are not made
By singing: "Oh, how beautiful!"
and sitting in the shade.'

RUDYARD KIPLING

HAPPY SNAPPER

My brand new, beautiful, black and silver 12 megapixel mini digital camera has just been pinched by my daughter. She promises to give it back, but I wonder. I'm told that it's desperately needed for an art project. Sound familiar? I bet I'll never see it again.

The happy snapper comes in two guises (apart from the camera snaffler above). The first type includes people

> '**There are no rules for good photographs; there are only good photographs.**'
>
> ANSEL ADAMS

like me (which means *most* people), who take few photos unless they're going somewhere special, and then they like to have a pocket-sized and user-friendly gadget that takes pictures in a second. They want something easy and reliable that will hook up to a computer so that the resulting shots can be edited and sent around the world to bore all their friends – who already know what they look like, and aren't particularly interested to see them in New York/ Paris/Val d'Isère or Mauritius. The best use for these types of picture is to set up your own digital photo frame (more later) that you can gaze at for hours, and that your friends can glance at quickly when they come to visit.

The second type of Happy Snapper is like my husband, so I know the breed well. They're happy only if they have the latest wizardry with which to take their pictures, and will stand for hours (in all weathers) on the touch-line, waiting for a goal, or at the bottom of a mountain waiting for their little darlings to get to the foot of the slalom run. And then they too will upload and email. This can work very well if they're taking shots of other people's darlings as well as their own. In any case, this style of Happy Snapper needs to have not just the camera, but all the lenses, tripods and filters to go with it. Watch out – he or she is an expensive person to buy for, and unless you're very careful, you'll probably get it wrong.

You'll notice that I'm not recommending specific kit here (perish the thought), but just great places to shop be-cause my suggestions would be quickly out of date. Having said that, if your Happy Snapper doesn't already have one, consider buying a digital photo frame – available in a wide price range – or a mini tripod. Retailers that offer these items are highlighted in the entries that follow. Alternative-ly, buy a copy of Photoshop Elements, a software package for editing pics, available from www.pcworld.co.uk and www.amazon.co.uk.

You can, of course, nip into your local branch of Jessops or even John Lewis to find a good range of photographic kit. However, if price is an issue, you're going to end up shopping online because that is, without question, where all the best deals are; and until the offline retailers realise that they need to compete, that's the way it will stay. Pocket the money you save and buy a treat for yourself as well.

Weatherproof camera case

www.cameras2u.com

This is an excellent place to find your next camera, and the site offers a lot of advice on digital photography. Couple this with free next-day delivery in the UK on orders over £100 and this is definitely somewhere you should visit.

Monster Pod

www.campkinsonline.com

For photographic enthusiasts this is a great place to shop. The excellent range includes digital SLRs and camcorders, and a speciality – compact digital cameras (some of which can be ordered in vibrant colours such as fuchsia pink, sizzling orange, wasabi green and bright red). Check out the Monster Pod – a mini digital camera tripod that sticks to just about everything. UK delivery; express available.

Digital SLRs

www.digitalfirst.co.uk

Here you'll find the latest cameras, including mini digitals, from all the major names – Pentax, Canon, Nikon, Olympus and Fuji – plus scanners and printers. Free UK mainland delivery and gift wrapping.

> **Did you know...**
> Modern digital cameras owe their development to US and Russian scientists in the 1960s. Satellites were launched to take photographs from space and beam pictures back to Earth without using film.

Digital photo frame

www.digitalframesdirect.com

Having been given a digital frame by my son for Christmas (yes, lucky me), I can definitely recommend them as a gift for any photographer. There's a very good range on offer here. UK delivery; express available.

Mini tripod

www.expansys.co.uk

This website, specialising in wireless technology, is a great place to find out about the latest mobile phones, smartphones, pocket PCs, sat nav systems and digital cameras. For some excellent gifts, check out the Ora and Cullmann tripods and accessories. Ships worldwide; express UK delivery.

Digital video camera

www.fotosense.co.uk

Fotosense offers an excellent range of the latest cameras,

plus MP3 players, binoculars, printers and studio lighting, from a list of over fifty manufacturers. They also have one of the UK's largest photographic accessory lists. UK delivery; express available.

Digital Zoom camera bag

www.morrisphoto.co.uk

The trouble with Happy Snappers is that they're constantly buying stuff. More and more lenses, filters and the like gradually make their way home, and – surprise, surprise – they seem to end up all over the house. The answer? Buy the best and biggest camera bag you can find, then try getting them to put their kit inside and keeping it where they can find it. Good luck! UK delivery.

Personalised photobook

www.photobox.co.uk

This website allows you to add your own favourite photo and title to personalise the cover of any of their albums. You can either fill it with photos yourself before giving it away – a really great personal gift that always goes down well – or leave it empty for the recipient to fill. Worldwide delivery.

Latest mega-pixel digi camera

www.pixmania.co.uk

Pixmania offers some of the best-priced cameras and in a variety of colours; so if you're thinking of giving your Happy Snapper a more expensive gift than usual, this is the place to have a look. Obviously, you'll want to give the best that you can afford and they'll give you all the information you need. Ships worldwide; express UK delivery.

Anything Leica

www.theclassiccamera.com

If your Happy Snapper has a Leica, this specialist retailer is *the* place to visit for a gift. The shop is full of the serious stuff, and if you're not absolutely sure about what you're buying, simply ask for advice. They stock everything Leica, plus Zeiss and Voigtlander lenses, Metz flashguns and Gitzo tripods. Worldwide delivery.

Did you know...

In 1973, a Kodak engineer called Steven Sasson developed the first digital camera. It weighed over 4 kg and had less than 0.1 megapixels. The technology has since come a long way in a very short time.

JEWEL COLLECTOR

*T*here are two Jewel Collectors in my family – my daughter and myself. We both love pretty jewellery, and believe me, if you're a collector, you can never have enough. I would love to be the kind of person who could just walk into Tiffany, Asprey or Bulgari and pick up something small, sparkling and special, but, like most people, I'm not, so I want to tell you how to be a bit cleverer with your shopping. Without a doubt, the best place in London to buy contemporary jewellery is Fenwicks in Bond Street, and if you're a jewellery collector who hasn't paid them a visit, you should do so as soon as possible. Alexis Bittar, Dana Kellin and Lisa Stewart are just some of the designers whose work is on offer. If you're not acquainted with them, you should become so immediately (and you'll also find them online at www.astleyclarke.com).

Pick carefully when buying jewellery as a gift: there are lots of different styles, from contemporary to classic by way of traditional. You can sometimes mix things up a bit by giving a contemporary floral motif piece to a classic person, but if you give something very traditional and 'pretty' to a modern jewellery collector, it'll go straight into the drawer or, even worse, be given to someone else. Think. Get it right. (And buy lots of treats for yourself as well!)

Kenneth Jay Lane animal print bangle
www.accessoriesonline.co.uk

Modern designer jewellery by the likes of Angie Gooderham, Les Néréides and Tarina Tarantino can be found here in an attractive and well-priced range. Look here when you want your next fashion jewellery fix, or when you're looking for a treat for a friend, and you definitely won't be disappointed. Worldwide delivery.

Robindira Undsworth designs
www.astleyclarke.com

This is the place to find special but accessibly priced jewellery by a group of designers you won't find together anywhere else. The cleverly chosen pieces are contemporary, wearable and utterly gorgeous. I particularly love the collection by Robindira Undsworth, which uses a variety of semi-precious stones. I'll have it all, thanks. Ships worldwide; express UK delivery and gift wrapping.

Crystal three-cone drop earrings
www.butlerandwilson.co.uk

Butler & Wilson's London store is famous for its signature whimsical fashion jewellery. You can choose online from a glamorous and well-priced range of necklaces, bracelets, earrings and brooches. Both costume jewellery and items using semi-precious stones (such as rose quartz, agate, amber and jade) are available. Worldwide delivery and gorgeous packaging.

White Fire silver star earrings
www.goldsmiths.co.uk

There's a wide range of jewellery here, including brands such as Emporio Armani, Argent and White Fire, and some great ideas for gifts. The watch selection includes many famous brand names, such as Tissot, Longines and Burberry. Expect delivery within three days.

Bespoke 10ct diamond ring
www.icecool.co.uk

Buy the perfect ring – if your budget will stretch that far. At Ice Cool you can select from a range of modern and classic well-priced jewels, including diamond studs, bracelets, pendants and rings. If you're looking for a real treat, give them a call and ask to speak to their diamond expert, who will design a piece specially for you. Ships worldwide.

Music note earrings by Tatty Devine
www.kabiri.co.uk
Kabiri carries an eclectic range of modern, international designers, such as Wendy Nichol, Adina, Carolina Bucci, Pippa Small and Tracy Matthews. The search facility on their website is excellent, as you can look by designer, type of jewellery and price. Worldwide delivery, including express.

Grey agate star necklace
www.lolarose.co.uk
Here's a beautiful and unusually designed website. Turn the pages of the book to find all the different colourways of the necklaces and bracelets made with rose quartz, white jade, green aventurine, mother of pearl and black agate. The prices for these beautifully designed pieces are very reasonable, so it's well worth having a look. Worldwide delivery.

Kinship green amethyst ring by Amitié
www.linksoflondon.com
Links of London are well known for selling a superb mix of jewellery in sterling silver and 18ct gold, plus cufflinks, pretty gifts and leather and silver accessories for your home. Each season they design a new collection of totally desirable pieces to tempt you with. Worldwide express delivery and gift wrapping.

Tomoko Furusawa wooden bead necklace
www.manjoh.com
On Manjoh's attractively designed contemporary jewellery website you'll find designers such as Izabel Camille, Vinnie Day, Benedicte Mouret and Scott Wilson, and the list is regularly expanded. Ships worldwide; express UK delivery plus gift wrapping.

Something really special
www.mingdesign.com
The designs here are really special, so this is not the place to find off-the-peg earrings, for example. However, if you are seeking out something really (and I mean *really*) gorgeous and different, take a look at the collections and commission something that will last for ever. You won't regret it. Worldwide delivery.

Pink amethyst drop earrings

www.pascal-jewellery.com

Here's a collection of timeless, stylish jewellery from a retailer that was originally established in Liberty of London about twenty-five years ago. You'll also find them in Harrods, Harvey Nichols and House of Fraser. The collection is updated at least four times a year, so you can be tempted regularly, and prices start at around £50. Worldwide delivery and gift wrapping.

Intervalle Indian sapphire cuff

www.swarovski.com

You've almost certainly heard of Swarovski and seen their beautifully laid-out shops full of glittering and stylish jewellery and accessories. A wide selection of their creations is available online, all set with their signature crystals and extremely hard to resist. Worldwide delivery and gift wrapping.

Tag Heuer F1 watch

www.thewatchhut.co.uk

If you're thinking of buying a watch as a gift, particularly online, take a look here, where there's an excellent selection of brands, some good prices and free next-day UK delivery.

Brands include Gucci, Tissot, Seiko, Hot Diamonds, Ebel and Maurice Lacroix. A Fat Face watch with red leather strap might also do the trick.

Elsa Peretti silver open heart charm

www.tiffany.com

Having bought one of these recently as a special gift for my daughter, I know how lovely and timeless they are. Although these hearts have been copied to death by others, I advise you not to be tempted by imitations. If you're going to buy, buy the real thing – she can only have one, after all. Ships worldwide; express UK delivery and gift wrapping.

Pilgrim flower and enamel earrings

www.treasurebox.co.uk

Here you'll find costume jewellery from Butler & Wilson, Tarina Tarantino, Barbara Easton, Angie Gooderham, Juicy Couture and Les Néréides to name just a few: they're adding new designers all the time. The emphasis is firmly on what's in fashion right now, so select jewellery to go with each new season's look. Ships worldwide; express UK delivery and gift wrapping.

KITCHEN GENIUS

*T*here are two serious cooks (other than me) in my family, and despite the fact that I've spent years preparing meals, I sometimes have to remind people that I can actually cook. (In fact, I spent a whole year learning to do so, and have a diploma to show for it.) I'll freely admit that I'm far happier if my husband (chef number 1) or eldest son (chef number 2) want to do the cooking. I'd just rather people didn't think that, because I haven't cooked Sunday lunch, I'm completely useless in the kitchen.

What to buy the kitchen genius in your life? Perhaps recipe books spring to mind, but I'm not recommending them here. It's so easy to find the latest book from Gordon Ramsey, Michel Roux or Jamie Oliver by yourself that you don't really need my help. Just remember that if you buy books online, you will, of course, find some excellent discounts, but don't leave ordering until the last minute or delivery might let you down.

There are some wonderful gifts you can buy for cookery lovers. The price range is huge, and you can spend a fortune, or not, as you please. The only problem will be deciding what to choose.

> *'Never eat more than you can lift.'*
> MISS PIGGY,
> *THE MUPPET SHOW*

Aga chalkstripe gauntlets

www.agacookshop.co.uk

Aga is a great British brand. If you know someone who has an Aga and likes cooking, this would be a great place to find them the latest cookery book or some of the attractive Aga textiles. Among the other products here are high-quality wooden chopping boards, bowls, chefs' knives and Kitchen Aid blenders. UK delivery.

Wine Course in a Box

www.ashburtoncookery-school.co.uk

Based in Ashburton in Devon, this cookery school offers one-day and one-week cookery courses, either of which would be a life-lasting gift. On the other hand, why not give their clever Wine Course in a Box instead? This includes wine, tasting glasses, glass phial wine aroma profiles, a professional wine appreciation manual and a tasting information booklet, plus a 'wine wheel' chart. UK delivery.

Extra virgin olive oil

www.carluccios.com

This site is a treasure trove of Italian ingredients, but bypass the gift sets (unless you really want to spend a great deal) and give a bottle of special olive oil instead – no cook can ever have enough. There are seasonal Italian specialities here as well. UK delivery.

Babel cake stand

www.conran.co.uk

If the person you're buying for loves contemporary rather than traditional designs, Conran is the place to head for. Most of the items here are totally modern, functional and often very attractive (if I sound surprised, it's because I'm definitely from the traditional side). Take a look around to find something fresh and original, like this black cake stand. Worldwide delivery and gift wrapping.

Wusthof knives

www.cooks-knives.co.uk

Here you can buy individual knives or sets by Global, Henckels, Sabatier, Haiku, Wusthof and more, together with professional knife sharpeners and OXO 'good grip' tools. My advice would be to buy knives only for someone you know really well, and to find out which set they're collecting before you buy. UK delivery.

Old Seattle coffee mugs

www.cucinadirect.com

You've got to be quite careful when you give china as it's unlikely to match what your recipient already has, so it has to be totally individual. These coffee mugs come in a set of six. They're robust and depict vintage American coffee advertisements. They're reasonably priced and would be great fun to use. Ships worldwide; express UK delivery and gift wrapping.

Eva Solo oil and vinegar carafes

www.diningstore.co.uk

Anything by award-winning Danish designer Eva Solo would look wonderful in a modern kitchen, and there's a very good choice here, from carafes and vases to coffee-makers and rice cookers. EU delivery.

Elephant tea caddies

www.divertimenti.co.uk

Divertiment is one of London's oldest cookery shops and has a huge range of gift ideas to browse through. I particularly love these unusual tall canisters designed with – yes, you guessed it – elephant motifs.

They're full of high-quality teas. Worldwide delivery.

Truffle gift box

www.oliviers-co.com

For those who love cooking and good food and want to use only the best, don't miss this wonderful site, offering special olive oils (infused with basil, lemon, chilli, mandarin or pepper), oil lamps, table cruets and other pantry goods. This company also has some very attractive gift selections. EU delivery.

One-day cookery course

www.rickstein.com

If you're buying for anyone who lives near Rick Stein's school in Padstow, Cornwall, a voucher for his one-day cookery course would make a great gift. Alternatively, his own collection of chef's linen, magnetic spice racks, wines or hampers full of his own products would be equally welcomed. Worldwide delivery for most items.

Alessi parrot corkscrew

www.saltandpepper.co.uk

Browse here if you are looking for a really well-designed online cookery store that doesn't bombard you with products but offers an excellent choice. There are some quite unusual brands alongside selections from the ranges by AGA, Le Creuset, Nigella Lawson and Bialetti, offering everything from bakeware and kitchen tools to pots, pans and small appliances. Delivers throughout the UK.

Peugeot Zephir electric pepper mill
www.silvernutmeg.com
As you might expect, Peugeot produces well-engineered and extremely attractive pepper mills, the like of which I haven't come across anywhere else. They are available in three colours. Silver Nutmeg offers plenty of gift ideas, including kettles, knives, pasta-makers, toasters, pancake pans, bread-making machines and much more. Worldwide delivery.

Simon Drew's witty aprons and tea towels
www.simondrew.co.uk
If your Kitchen Genius has a ready wit, you can't go far wrong with this entertaining range of accessories and non-sense from Simon Drew, an artist based in Devon. His de-

signs are widely available, but if you want something specific, it is easiest to order direct. His themes include lines such as, Moled Wine, Last Mango in Paris, and Dinersaurs. Make sure you know what makes your genius laugh. Worldwide delivery.

Oakwood chop 'n' pour hachoir set
www.thecookingshop.co.uk
This unusual set consists of a solid oak bowl with a steel chopper. The idea is that you chop your herbs in the bowl, then pour them straight into your cooking pan without spilling. You'll also find knife blocks, salmon boards, preserving pans, oil drizzlers and lots of other ideas here. Worldwide delivery.

William Bounds chocolate mill
www.thecookskitchen.com
This is an excellent, innovative idea that prevents your warm fingers from melting the chocolate as it's grated. Also look at the sections devoted to linen and kitchen utensils for fun retro designs and colourful bar sets. Worldwide delivery and gift wrapping.

PAMPERED PRINCESS

*O*f course the Pampered Princess can be just about any age, and it seems to me that most members of the female sex love pampering of one sort or another at any time of the year, not just for birthdays, Mother's Day and so on. What most Princesses love are the pampering treats that, luckily for you, do not have to be that expensive. A pretty pot of Benefit lip balm, the latest shade of Bobbie Brown eye shadow, or a bottle of Molton Brown shower gel will always bring a lift to this girl. The important thing to remember is to keep on pampering her again and again. I know these things.

Wickle eau de parfum
www.austique.co.uk

This is an attractive boutique on the King's Road in London, and its online store offers a bit of everything: modern jewellery, lingerie, accessories, Rococo chocolates, and unusual bathtime treats, such as Limoncello Body Butter and Arnaud Chamomile and Lavender Bubble Bath. Ships worldwide; express delivery and gift wrapping available.

Essence of John Galliano candle
www.beautique.com

Beautique is a well-designed hair and beauty website. Among the many brands it sells are Aveda, Bumble & Bumble, Dermologica, Dr Hauschka, Carole Franck, Guerlain and Jean-Charles Brosseau. The home page has lots of special offers, so it's well worth having a look around. Express UK delivery and gift wrapping.

Almond lip scrub by Sara Happ

www.cocoribbon.com

Calling itself London's lifestyle boutique, Coco Ribbon offers a selection of contemporary clothing by designers such as Collette Dinnigan, Rebecca Taylor and Cynthia Vincent. Here you can find pretty lingerie and swimwear, plus a small but beautiful range of handbags and jewellery. Worldwide delivery and gift wrapping.

Make-up purse by Lulu Guinness

www.hqhair.com

If you haven't used this site already, you should try it. This fun and incredibly useful beauty product retailer offers chic cosmetic ranges, marvellous hair products and contemporary skincare. You'll discover exquisite cosmetic bags by Kate Spade and Lulu Guinness, perfect for presents and also for treats. Worldwide and UK express delivery, plus gift wrapping.

Orange and honey custard box

www.savonneriesoap.com

This is a beautiful website, with an extremely luxurious feel. Here you can buy exquisitely packaged hand-made soaps (think Flower Garden and Honey Cake), bath and body products, such as geranium and bergamot oil, perfect gift boxes and The Naughty Weekend Kit – take a look and you'll find out. UK delivery.

Belle Fleur white orchid tea candle

www.spacenk.co.uk

Nars, Stila, Darphin, Diptyque, Laura Mercier, Eve Lom, Frederic Fekkai and Dr Sebagh are just some of the sixty-plus brands offered by this retailer, famous for bringing unusual and hard-to-find products to the UK. It's also an excellent place for gifts as they offer a personalised message and gift-wrapping service, plus next-day delivery if you need it. Ships worldwide.

'I really want to play Princess Leia...'

EWAN MCGREGOR

SPORTING GENIUS

I thought about creating different characters for each and every sport covered in this section, but there are just too many to include. The shops and sites listed are, in my opinion, the best places to buy gifts for those interested in sport (and Calum - you've taught me much of what I know!). I've focused on what seem to me to be the most popular sports, each of which needs its own range of equipment, and tried to inspire you with a few gift ideas. I'm sure you can come up with even more.

I have one important tip, which I'll mention only once (be thankful for that). Don't splash out on expensive equipment unless you're *absolutely sure* it's the right sort. If you want to be generous, it's far better to give a gift voucher, no matter how boring that might seem. When handing it over you could say, for example, 'I wanted to give you a set of clubs/new fishing rod/posh bike, but I thought you'd probably get more fun out of choosing your own.' Trust me on this – I've learnt the hard way.

As the year goes by, listen out for hints from your sporting genius about gear that he or she would love to own if only it wasn't so expensive/extravagant. Make a note of them in the back of this book and consult it when the time comes. You can't go wrong if you buy something that they're already lusting after.

Among the gift ideas for the most popular sports, I've also included some thoughts about croquet (for that lovely flat lawn), table tennis (even though you may always be beaten) and snooker (why do they always lose the balls?). Enjoy.

You might be wondering what qualifies me to choose sports gifts, so I'll tell you. In my family I have had four rugby fanatics (and one ex-player), two fishermen, three golfers, five skiers, two shots, three ex-cricketers, two horse-riders (one of those was me), three tennis players, five croquet players, four snooker players, three gym members and one pilates trainee. You should feel reassured.

The gifts are divided into the following categories, and I'm sure you'll work out who is who in your own circle of friends and relatives:

Fitness Fanatics ● Downhill Racers ● Wet Bobs ● Caught on the Fly ● Hole in One ● Saddle Up ● Racket Addicts ● Match of the Day ● In the Garden

Dear Lord, in the battle that goes on through life
I ask but a field that is fair,
A chance that is equal with all in the strife,
A courage to strive and to dare;
And if I should win, let it be by the code
With my faith and my honor held high;
And if I should lose, let me stand by the road,
And cheer as the winners go by.

FROM 'PRAYER OF A SPORTSMAN'
BERTON BRALEY

FITNESS FANATICS
GYM, PILATES, RUNNING, YOGA

Adidas sports bag by Stella McCartney
www.adidas-shop.co.uk

Almost anything in the Stella McCartney for Adidas range would make an excellent gift for a fitness/gym fanatic. This is quite an expensive collection, but the clothing combines functionality, design and quality to make each piece special. The range is available online and from most good sports shops. UK express delivery.

Zip hoody and pants
www.elliegray.com

This is an excellent sportswear site. Offering brands such as USA Pro, Pure Lime and Deha as well as their own, you'll find a selection of hoodies and jackets, sweatshirts, outerwear, sports bras and accessories in a range of styles. Ships worldwide; express UK delivery.

Reebok elliptical cross-trainer
www.fitness-superstore.co.uk

I'm including just one equipment superstore in case you're feeling generous and thinking of buying a treadmill or other hefty machine for someone. This site also has a very good selection of smaller equipment, such as gym balls and ab trainers. UK delivery.

Anything by McKenzie or Lee Rock
www.jdsports.co.uk

As one of the largest UK sports retailers, this site offers a huge

Adidas shoes were developed in Germany in 1920 by Adi Dassler, the man who gave them his name. Their popularity was assured when, in 1932, Arthur Jonath wore them for his bronze-medal-winning 100-metre run in the Los Angeles Olympics; and in 1936 Jesse Owens won four gold medals in the Berlin Olympics while wearing them.

range of sports shoes and gear on its website, including brands such as Lacoste, Nike, Puma, Reebok and Adidas. The clothing ranges are extensive, and the ordering system is extremely easy to use. Worldwide and UK express delivery.

Acceleration trainer
www.powerplate.com
You might well have heard of these vibrating machines, and seen them in John Lewis or on television. According to the website, the PowerPlate® activates muscle contractions in the body multiple times per second. It was first used by Soviet cosmonauts in the 1960s to counteract the bone and muscle degeneration caused by zero gravity. In 1999 the Dutch Olympic trainer Guus van der Meer adapted it for elite athletes, and then for people of all ages, weights and fitness levels. My advice? If you can afford it – prices start around £1000 – buy one now. Forget all the jokes: this machine really works.

Shanghai Milea Mesh shoe
www.puma.com
Puma have now launched their own website and offer almost

their full range online. The shoe I've chosen is one of the most fashion-forward and yes, you've guessed, I have a pair. EU delivery, with express option available other than at peak times.

Casall strap top and rib puff pants
www.sportswoman.co.uk
Casall offers sports clothing for fitness, golf, tennis, running and other activities. The fitness range in particular is very different from what you can find elsewhere. Contemporary colours and styles combine to create a totally original collection. It also sells a small range of sports accessories, such as yoga mats. Ships worldwide; express UK delivery.

SB yoga bag and flowered yoga mat
www.sweatybetty.com
At the fast-growing sportswear retailer Sweaty Betty there's a really stylish range of clothing for fitness training, as well as sleek (and minimal) beachwear, chic and well-priced skiwear, and accessories such as leg and arm warmers and books on yoga. Worldwide delivery; postage is free on orders over £50 in the UK.

Deluxe yoga kit
www.yogastudio.co.uk

This site has one of the largest collections of yoga kit available online. With a wide range of products that you can buy individually (such as mats, belts and bags) and a variety of yoga and pilates kits from basic to advanced, it's a perfect gift destination. Express delivery in the UK.

Pilatina T-shirt
www.wellicious.com

Well-being lifestyle brand Wellicious offers chic and sexy clothes for yoga and pilates on one of the most attractive websites around. Its range includes T-shirts, satin pants, jackets and ballet bodies, plus yoga pants and catsuits. Ships worldwide. First-class and express delivery in the UK.

DOWNHILL RACER
SKIING, SNOWBOARDING

Technical baselayer
www.blacks.co.uk

Skiing kit is extremely expensive: I know this only too well because I've collected five sets for members of my family over the years. I also know that come the ski season, they all want new 'stuff' in this season's colours. Technical baselayer tops are hideously expensive, but make great gifts for skiers. Express UK delivery.

Oakley iridium goggles
www.ellis-brigham.com

Ellis Brigham offers brands such as North Face, Ice Breaker, Patagonia and Lowe Alpine. Every possible type of equipment is clearly shown on the website, and there are some good sports gift ideas as well, including items by Maglite, Leatherman, Victorinox and Toollogic. Ships worldwide.

Brambleberry draw-cord fleece jacket
www.llbean.com

L.L. Bean is an American company that always has an excellent range of fleeces and outerwear, including jackets, hats and gloves, some of them in fine cashmere, that you won't find anywhere else. There are winter gifts galore here. Worldwide express delivery.

Snow Ski Joe Bender
www.nevisport.com

OK, I know what you're going to say: this is a totally daft and useless toy, but it is cute, and it would be a good stocking filler for a young (or old) skier. Joe Bender is a bendy wire character attached to a magnetic base, and can be posed any way you want. (Benders are available for other sports too.) Nevisport is a great place to shop for ski gear and clothing, whether you visit one of their stores or shop online. UK delivery.

Fleece
www.patagonia.com

Patagonia specialises in equipment for alpine skiing, rock climbing, Nordic climbing and fly fishing, so you won't be surprised that they offer a collection of really high-tech, highly insulated products. Nothing is inexpensive, but you can be sure you're buying the best. Ships worldwide; express UK delivery.

White Rock Balascarfa
www.simplypiste.co.uk

This gift idea is a clever all-in-one scarf, balaclava and hat, and there are ten different ways it can be worn. It's perfect for skiing because it's neat (better than shoving your hat in your pocket) and the balaclava option is terrific if a blizzard should strike. Ships worldwide; express UK delivery.

Camelbak Mule
www.snowandrock.com

In the gift and gadget section of Snow+Rock you'll find lots of ideas, including books and films, watches, two-way radios, solar chargers and compasses, plus a full range of equipment, clothing and accessories by brands such as Animal, Ski Jacket, Billabong, Helly Hanson, O'Neill, Quicksilver, Salomon and Oakley. Ships worldwide; express UK delivery.

Burton Gig snowboard bag
www.summits.co.uk

Summits is a great place to shop for skiers and snowboarders as it not only offers a good range of clothing from brands such as Helly Hanson, North Face and Columbia, but also has a very strong range of skis, boards, boots, bags and bindings. I like the concise information they provide about everything shown on the site. UK delivery.

WET BOBS

DIVING, ROWING, SAILING, WATERSKIING

Super Le Tube

www.andark.co.uk

Andark are based in Southampton, and offer loads of stuff for the watersports enthusiast, from ride-on tubes and power kites to a full range of watersports clothing, inflatable dinghies, wetsuits and diving equipment, waterskis, torches, knives and underwater camera accessories. (They also sell equestrian clothing.) Express UK delivery.

Jungle swim shorts

www.crewclothing.co.uk

Crew has a really attractive and modern store, with a constantly expanding range. It offers all the Crew gear, from the full collection of sailing-inspired clothing to specialist footwear, faux fur jackets and gilets, and excellent travel bags, gloves, hats and socks. Ships worldwide; express UK delivery.

Striped hoody

www.henrilloydstore.com

For the sailor this is a great place to browse, offering stylish sailing clothing for guys and girls, footwear, luggage and specific branded marinewear. You can't buy their technical sailing gear online, but the collection is chic, stylish and not overpriced. Delivers worldwide.

Lighthouse lamp

www.nautical-living.co.uk

This is not so much a sailing store as a great place to find gifts for anyone who likes the nautical lifestyle. There are cupboards, coffee tables, lamps, mirrors, duvet covers, fabrics, picture frames, towels, pegs, light-pulls and lots more – all with a sailing theme, and all beautifully photographed. UK delivery.

Definition of a coarse sailer: 'One who, in a crisis, forgets nautical language and shouts, "For God's sake, turn left!"'

MICHAEL GREEN

The first SCUBA (self-contained underwater breathing apparatus) equipment was the aqualung, co-developed by Jacques-Yves Cousteau and Emile Gagnanin the 1940s. A charismatic Frenchman and conservationist, Cousteau was also the first to bring images of underwater marvels to our television screens in the 1960s, inspiring a new generation of divers in the process.

Sailing print or poster

www.postershop.co.uk

Those who are addicted to living or spending time, on or by the water usually love to surround themselves with reminders of their favourite places and adventures. There are some wonderful sailing prints to be found here, most of which would make excellent gifts. Worldwide delivery.

Pirate alarm clock

www.purplemarine.com

Purple Marine offers a full range of sailing gear for the keen sailor – everything from bilge pumps and hatches to chart-holders, boat-covers and buoyancy aids. There's an enormous choice. Ships worldwide; express UK delivery.

Fun T-shirt

www.rock-the-boat.co.uk

A visit to this store is essential if you know anyone who rows.

It has all the gear, plus funny T-shirts and tops that only those with rowers in the family will understand: for example, 'Ergo, Ergoing, Ergone' and 'Going Forwards Backwards'. All great gifts for the rower you know. Delivers throughout the EU; express UK delivery.

Optimum sailing watch

www.sailingclothingstore. co.uk

The Isle of Wight is a mecca for sailors and the perfect location for this store, but the website is easier to reach for those who don't happen to live there. Musto, Henri Lloyd and Gill are the three main brands on offer here, and they include clothing, accessories, footwear and luggage ranges. You'll also find deck shoes and chandlery, Leatherman knives, Silva compasses and charts, and marine books. EU delivery.

CAUGHT ON THE FLY

Ode to the Fisherman
Behold the fisherman:
He riseth up in the morning,
Disturbeth the whole household.
Mighty are his preparations.
He goes forth full of hope.
When the day is far spent
He returneth, smelling of strong drink,
and the truth not in him. (ANON)

Just a word of advice here: fishing is a seriously serious sport – you don't stand in the river in the freezing cold and driving rain for hours at a time with (probably) little hope of catching anything unless you really love it. Don't try to find the fisherman you know a silly gift – he is unlikely to appreciate it. Buy him something useful and you'll be popular for evermore.

Voyager hip flask
www.dalvey.com
Dalvey specialise in gifts for sportsmen, but also offer travel and business accessories. An essential gift for any fisherman is a hip flask, and here you'll find a small but beautiful choice, including the compass-set Voyager Expedition Flask. Worldwide delivery.

Fishing tackle kit
www.fly-fishing-tackle. co.uk
Everything for the keen fisherman is available here, from a full range of rods and reels to waders, hats, caps and gloves. Go straight past the fly-tying kits, unless you're sure they'll be welcome, and focus instead on fly boxes, tackle bags, rod carriers, fly-tying tools, lamps and magnifiers. Ships worldwide; express UK delivery.

Hardy marksman net
www.johnnorris.co.uk
This company, which is based in Cumbria, supplies fishing equipment and accessories by Snowbee, Orvis, Musto, Greys, Le Chameau, Daiwa, Barbour

and lots more. Why have I chosen the net? Well, you have to assume that the fisherman in your life *will* catch something, sometime. Also on offer is a full range of shooting accessories, from gun-cleaning kits to shooting sticks. Worldwide delivery.

Tape measure zinger
Orvis.co.uk

Founded in 1856, Orvis is one of the oldest mail-order companies in the USA, and is now well established in the UK too. It offers everything for the fisherman, whether the quarry is Atlantic salmon, pike or still-water trout. There's also a range of luggage and travel items, men's and women's clothing, and an excellent array of equipment for pets. Ships worldwide; express UK delivery.

Salmon fishing bone china mug
www.tackleshop.co.uk

If someone you know is interested in carp, coarse, game, match, pike, pole or sea fishing, you must take a look at this site because the product range is extremely comprehensive. A pair of chest waders (for the fly fisherman in your life who needs a new pair) is a handy gift idea. Clothing and accessories are also available. Ships worldwide; delivery charges are reasonable.

Silver salmon cufflinks
www.thecooljewelshop. co.uk

Here you can find cufflinks relating to just about any sport. There are also designs for car, motorbike, train, theatre and music enthusiasts. Most of the cufflinks are from sterling silver and are very reasonably priced. Nine-carat gold versions are also available in some designs. Free worldwide delivery on orders over £50.

101 Golden Rules of Fishing
www.amazon.co.uk

This beautifully presented book by Rob Beattie is perfect for both new and experienced fishermen. As well as lots of hints and tips (which the expert might not thank you for), it tells you: 'How to deal with an angry bailiff', 'How to fish somewhere that's never been fished before', and offers plenty of fishing wit and wisdom. Ships worldwide; express UK delivery and gift wrapping.

HOLE IN ONE

Golf TV Leadbetter Interactive

www.clickgolf.co.uk

This is a very quick and easy site to use, although, like most of the golfing websites, it's very busy and offers a range of products that at first sight looks almost too much. You can find top brand names, such as Callaway and Mizuna, and some very good special offers, plus lots of gift ideas. World-wide and express UK delivery.

Box of Big Bertha balls by Callaway

www.directgolf.co.uk

Direct Golf is a store for the serious golfer, and there are plenty of gift ideas here; though this is definitely not a 'golfer's gift store' as such. There's equipment by Callaway, Wilson, Nike, Mizuno, MacGregor and many more, clothing by Nike, Adidas, Ashworth. EU and UK express delivery.

'I know I am getting better at golf because I am hitting fewer spectators.'

GERALD FORD

'Golf is like a love affair. If you don't take it seriously, it's no fun; if you do take it seriously, it breaks your heart.'

GEORGE COLE AS ARTHUR DALEY IN *MINDER*

Gleneagles golf umbrella

www.gleneagles.com

There is only one Gleneagles Hotel, and it produces its own range of embroidered clothing. I wouldn't choose that as a gift unless the intended recipient had actually played there, but there are lots of other gift ideas on this site. Take a look at the very good range of golfing accessories and you're bound to find something appropriate. Worldwide delivery.

Digital range finder

www.golf-gift.co.uk

There are some extremely useful gift ideas here, ranging from the sensible (trolleys, range finders and core counters) to the silly (donkey head club-covers and exploding, flashing or unputtable golf balls). Many of the items here would make great stocking fillers, although there are also well-priced bags and trolleys too. Worldwide delivery.

Golf gloves
www.hattiesmart.com
Hattie Smart designs golf gloves, but they are far from run-of-the-mill. These are designer golf gloves, made from the finest leather, and available in a range of colours, including pistachio, violet, fuchsia and cranberry for women, and kangaroo, bay leaf and vanilla for men. Worldwide delivery and gift wrapping.

Groover
www.118golf.co.uk
Here you will find a diverse range of products for the golfer, many of which will make excellent gifts. Check out the accessories and gadgets, such as swing trainers and ball retrievers, and the interesting array of DVDs and books. The excellent delivery service offers a range of options.

PGA Tour Perfect Touch practice net
www.onlinegolf.co.uk
This is a typical sports site with loads and loads of products and brand names, from Nike and Wilson to Adidas and Pringle. It includes golf clubs, bags, clothing, shoes and other accessories for both men and women. It even sells gold balls. There is also a very good range for the junior golfer. Worldwide delivery.

Automatic putting system
www.planetgolfuk.co.uk
Although most golfers are very 'serious' about their game, golf can by played by people of any age and ability, and for fun as well. This putting system, which has an automatic ball return, could be given as a stocking filler at Christmas, or as a gift at any time, and can be used practically anywhere. Ships worldwide.

Golfing Wit
www.waterstones.com
So what do golfers like to read? Well, apart from biographies of their favourite famous golfer, there is a wealth of silly, sometimes useful and often totally daft books on offer. I particularly like this one by Aubrey Malone. Subtitled 'Quips and quotes for the golf obsessed', it doesn't pretend to be clever; it's just amusing and light-hearted. Ships worldwide; express UK delivery and gift wrapping.

SADDLE UP

Hunter wellies
www.dragonflysaddlery.co.uk

This unique saddlery is based in the wonderful town of Ditchling, Sussex. Here you can choose from army camouflage jodphurs, Buddies 'jods' and Saddlehuggers in loads of different colours. Then there are long and short jodhpur boots, body protectors, wellies, muck boots and rainproof jackets. Hunter is a high-quality welly brand and quite expensive, but a very good gift for a rider – provided you know the right size. UK delivery.

Striped polo shirt
www.joulesclothing.com

Joules is a clothing website with a difference. Beautifully photographed and well laid out, it has fun, sporty separates for just about everyone – provided you and yours happen to like stripes and colours. It's aimed mainly at the riding fraternity, although many of the clothes, particularly the jackets and fleeces, would have a much wider appeal, and can frequently be seen on those who almost certainly are never to be found near a horse. World-wide delivery.

Two Ways to Get in Shape to Own a Horse

(from 'Ten Ways to Get in Shape to Own a Horse')

1 Drop a heavy steel object on your foot. Don't pick it up right away. Shout 'Get off, stupid! Get off!'

2 Lie face down in the mud in your most expensive riding clothes and repeat to yourself: 'This is a learning experience, this is a learning experience...'

Peppermint pony holdall
www.mad4ponies.com

This neon-bright website is just for youngsters (girls really) aged 5–16, who love to ride. It has funky pink or purple nubuck boots, glitter whips, vibrant grooming kits, sparkly diamanté hat covers, colourful jodhpurs, bright and brilliant products for a favourite pony, and a variety of horse-related gifts and games. Ships world-wide; express UK delivery.

Loveson chaps
www.theequestrianstore. com

This well-designed and easy-to-navigate website sells just about everything for horse and rider. You'll find a com-prehensive clothing section offering jodphurs and hard hats, jackets and boots; and in the horse section you'll find saddles, bridles, horse rugs, training aids, grooming and stable equipment, and a wide range of accessories. Express worldwide delivery.

RACKET ADDICT

Babolat racket bag
www.directsports-eshop. co.uk

Direct Sports is aimed at the tennis, badminton or squash player and offers brands such as Head, Wilson, Yonex and Babolat to name but a few. There's a very good racket se-lector here as well, but you'd be wise to find out what the recipi-ent wants before splashing out. UK delivery.

Dunlop eight dozen trainer bucket
www.originalsports.co.uk

This is another excellent sports website, with rackets by Prince, Wilson, Babolat and Yonex amongst others, plus ball baskets and ball lobbers by Lobster, Tennis Tower and Shotmaker. In fact, it seems to have everything for the tennis enthusiast. Ships worldwide; express UK delivery.

'In tennis the addict moves about a hard rectangle and seeks to ambush a fuzzy ball with a modified snow-shoe.'
ELLIOT CHAZE

Trionz dual loop magnetic ion therapy bracelet

www.pdhsports.com

This Midlands-based racket specialist offers equipment and clothing for tennis, squash, badminton, racketball and hockey from all the major brands. UK delivery.

Own the Zone vibration dampeners

www.pwp.com

There's a great deal here for court-game enthusiasts, with rackets by Wilson, Dunlop, Head, Slazenger and Prince, well-priced tennis balls and tennis shoes, and lots of accessories, including the ITP series of DVDs. Ships worldwide; express UK delivery.

Gift certificate

www.racquetlink.com

This website offers rackets by Prince, Wilson, Babolat and Yonex, amongst others. It also sells ball baskets and lobbers by Lobster, Tennis Tower and Shotmaker, plus everything else for the tennis player. There are so many gift ideas here that I suggest you give your racket addicts a gift certificate and let them choose for themselves. You could, of course,

'Good shot, bad luck, and hell are the five basic words to be used in a game of tennis, though these, of course, can be slightly amplified.'

VIRGINIA GRAHAM'
SAY PLEASE

go for the tennis bookends… Ships worldwide; express UK delivery.

Wristbands

www.sportswoman.co.uk

At this beautifully photographed website you can find the Cassall range of sportwear, which includes tennis clothes ranging from designer dresses to wristbands. As long as you know your player's size, you won't go far wrong here. Everything is very good quality, and although it's not cheap, it's not overpriced either. Ships worldwide; express UK delivery available.

MATCH OF THE DAY
CRICKET, FOOTBALL, RUGBY

The Bumper Book of Football
www.amazon.co.uk

Beautifully designed and illustrated, Hunter Davies' book is perfect gift for any lover of football. It contains lots of facts and anecdotes about every possible aspect of the 'world's most popular game' – how it began and developed; stories about great clubs, managers and players; and descriptions of epic games. There are lots of books about football, but this has to be one of the best. Ships worldwide; express delivery and gift wrapping.

Cricket bat flask
www.cricketbits.co.uk

This is the one-stop-shop for cricket novelties and gifts, with bestsellers such as a cricket-ball clock, cricket letter rack and a framed, limited edition picture commemorating 'The Birth of the Ashes' in 1882, showing the handwritten batting orders, scorecard and original scorer's sheet. Delivers throughout the UK.

Puma FIFA football
www.kitbag.co.uk

Kitbag is one of the best websites for football and rugby clothing, equipment and accessories. It's clear and quick to get round, has a really wide range of products, and offers fast delivery worldwide.

Kookaburra junior cricket set
www.owzat-cricket.co.uk

This online retailer sells bats by Gunn & Moore, Kookaburra and Gray-Nichols, plus loads of other brands. You'll also find gloves, pads, kitbags, body protection, accessories and balls. EU and express UK delivery.

'In 1823, William Webb Ellis first picked up the ball in his arms and ran with it. And for the next 156 years forwards have been trying to work out why.'
SIR TASKER WATKINS, PRESIDENT OF THE WORLD RUGBY UNION.

Favourite team shirt

www.rugbymegastore.com

This is just as it sounds: a huge, busy website offering a total range for the rugby player, including bags, balls, team kit, books and rugby boots by brands such as Mizuno, Puma, Adidas and Nike. Check out the physio bag – it will probably be needed. UK delivery.

Legends of Rugby – limited signed editions

www.rugbyrelics.com

Rugby Relics is a family business based in north Wales, and has an amazing collection of rugby gifts and memorabilia, including signed photos, programmes, magazines and shirts, many of which can be supplied with a certificate of authenticity. If you want to buy a gift for a rugby-mad friend, you won't go wrong if you start your search here. Ships worldwide; express UK delivery.

Bronco Mini Goal

www.sweatbandoutdoor.co.uk

Most footballers, big and small, like to have something to aim their football at so that it doesn't travel too far away and take ages to retrieve (or so I'm told). This mini goal is the perfect answer. It can be used on just about any surface, and it fits on the back seat of a car. UK delivery.

Favourite team kit

www.uksoccershop.com

Although I have only rugby players in my family, they all watch football too, and I know that anything from their favourite team's strip goes down well at present-giving time. My only advice here is to make sure you are buying for the right team, as giving something in the wrong colours is far worse than giving nothing at all! Ships worldwide; express UK delivery on some items.

'Remember that rugby is a team game; all 14 of you make sure you pass the ball to Jonah.'

ANONYMOUS FAX TO THE NEW ZEALAND RUGBY TEAM IN 1995 WHEN KIWI JONAH LOMU BECAME A LEGEND

IN THE GARDEN

The two online stores below offer a comprehensive range of equipment for great garden games. Just make sure that the recipient of that wonderful Jacques croquet set has a lawn they're happy to play on, otherwise you could be in trouble.

Kettler Champion Go-Kart
www.gardengames.co.uk
Trampolines, climbing frames, swings, ride-ons and remote-controlled cars are just some of the products you can order here. This site offers speedy UK delivery and will also ship to the USA, Canada and Spain.

Jacques croquet set
www.mastersgames.com
Here you'll find a wide range of traditional indoor and outdoor games made of high-quality materials, including Jacques croquet sets, lawn bowls, deck quoits, skittles, baccarat and giant chess. Ships worldwide; express UK delivery.

'HINTS UPON CROQUET'
BY A COMMITTEE OF CROAKERS FROM *THE QUEEN: THE LADY'S NEWSPAPER AND COURT CIRCULAR*, AUGUST 1868

When you arrive at the lawn look over the implements, and if there is a crooked or crazy mallet among them, or a ball that is cracked or bruised, or not well turned, take care not to be on the side to which these belong. Perhaps they have been provided on purpose, and do not you be the victim.

Ladies have an easy and ready means of assisting their partners and themselves. They need only to stand over the balls, and shuffle them along with their feet – a very common practice, and a very effective one.

Talking to people while they are playing is a very effective check to their progress, and leads them to make oversights from which you will derive advantage. A dispute upon some point of the game, or a good story, or a bit of scandal, or a mere joke, will sometimes secure you a victory.

VOYAGER

*W*e all know plenty of people who love to travel. The Voyager is never totally happy unless he or she has a destination in prospect and is ready to start packing. The problem when buying gifts for travel addicts is that there are so many different kinds. (One extreme is the Adventurer, and you can find plenty of gift ideas for him or her on pages 114–17.)

There are certain things I *need* to take with me when I travel, wherever I go (apart from far too many clothes and pairs of shoes, that is), so that's the list I'm giving you here. Some are geared more to women than men, while others will do for both sexes. Buy them for yourself to try them out, and then you'll know exactly what your travelling friend will really appreciate.

'The world is a book, and those who do not travel, read only a page.'
ST AUGUSTINE

Power Monkey
www.addonsworld.co.uk
This is an amazing little gizmo, basically a high-powered battery that holds its charge for up to a year. You charge up at home, then use it when you're away to recharge your mobile phone, iPod, digital camera

and all your other indispensable gadgets. What more could the seasoned traveller ask for? UK express delivery.

Irox Global Radio-controlled Travel Clock
www.essentials4travel. co.uk

Irix produces a multi-band travel alarm clock that synchronises automatically with global time transmitters. This is just one of the huge range of travellers' essentials stocked on this website, which includes adaptors, portfolios, backpacks, golf bags and lots more. Worldwide delivery; free in UK for orders of £19 and over.

Ultimate Ears Super. fi 3 Studio Headphones
www.headphoneworld. co.uk

This is a seriously good set of headphones, excellent for the traveller who doesn't want to go anywhere without an iPod or MP3 player. Amongst the huge range of goods on offer here you will also find adaptors so that you can plug your headphones into your mobile phone too. Ships worldwide; express UK delivery.

Power Traveller iPod Speaker
www.iskins.co.uk

I'm a real fan of these amazing, tiny iPod speakers that are small enough to fit in your handbag: I can't recommend them highly enough. They are very much smaller than most of the other speakers you can find, make a really good sound and are genuinely worth the money. Buy the Gear 4 Fire-Power World Tour Charger here too with international adaptors. Ships worldwide; express UK delivery.

Silva pocket binoculars
www.itchyfeet.com

I love Itchy Feet – the store that was started by a couple of adventure addicts. It's a great source of travel clothing and essentials aimed at everyone from novices taking their first adventure holiday to old hands looking for the latest developments in travel equipment. It stocks ranges by Patagonia, Berghaus, North Face, Mountain Hardwear, Camelbak and more, selling everything from base layers to down jackets, adaptors and mosquito nets. Ships worldwide; express UK delivery.

Longchamp large Pliage bag

www.longchamp.com

The Pliage is a really great hold-all. Made of leather-trimmed canvas, it folds down into the size of a large envelope. Every traveller should have one. You can call Longchamp in London and ask them to send you one, or buy the slightly smaller size at BA's HighLife Shop at www.highlifeshop.com. The largest size is 55 x 40 x 23 cm. Call to order. UK delivery.

Antler Urbanite Trolley Backpack

www.looksluggage.co.uk

This is an incredibly light, contemporary wheeled backpack, with a telescopic handle and loads of pockets, including a 'wet' one. It's great as hand luggage, or just for toting stuff around when you don't want to have an extra bag on your arm. Indispensable. UK delivery.

Multi-function clock

www.magellans.co.uk

Magellans is the largest travel supply store in the USA, but now has a British outlet. Their selection is wonderful: luggage and totes by PacSafe, Case Logic and others that are sometimes hard to find; also everything else the Voyager could possibly need for travel, including clothing, toiletry kits, padlocks and tags. All orders are shipped from the USA, but duty is included. Worldwide delivery.

Eagle Creek Pro-Tech Cube

www.rohan.co.uk

Eagle Creek make some of the best travel accessories going, so if you know someone who likes to be organised when they travel, buy them this fleece-lined pack to keep their chargers, digital camera, mini speakers and any other small gizmos all together in one place. There are lots of other excellent ideas on this site as well. Ships worldwide. express UK delivery.

Rough Guides

www.roughguides.com

The Rough Guides are great: they cover more than 200 countries, including most of Europe and the USA, over half of Africa, and most of Asia and Australasia. Hotel recommendations range from budget to luxury. On this website you can see all the guides and maps together in one place. Worldwide delivery.

Parlux 3500 Super Compact hairdryer

www.saloneasy.co.uk

For anyone who travels in the UK or Europe, this hairdryer is a must. Professional brand Parlux have the best selection of high-powered dryers, none of which is available on the high street. They come in lots of colours, such as pink, silver or red. If you travel a lot in the USA, order from www.amazon. com so that it's waiting when you arrive. Ships worldwide.

Safari bag

www.sandstormbags.com

Sandstorm is the only range of authentic, premium safari-style bags out of Africa. Hand-made in Kenya, they are perfect for your next safari, but also ideal for walking in the Cotswolds or taking on a weekend break in a five-star hotel! They look good anywhere, delivering a striking combination of luxury, style and durability. Ships world-wide; express UK delivery.

Blue Kimono Jewellery Roll by Cris Notti

www.therenovationstore. co.uk

US designer Cris Notti has created an unusual collection of make-up cases, jewellery rolls, sleep masks and travel totes in a variety of patterns, including authentic kimono fabrics. It's a wonderful collection that you can't find anywhere else, and is great for the traveller. Worldwide delivery plus gift wrapping.

JetRest luxury travel pillow

www.travelwithcare.com

This fleece-covered neck pillow is a must for anyone who takes long plane or train journeys. The huge range of travel goods on this site also includes sleeping bags, wheeled luggage, padlocks, money belts, torches and multi tools. You will find ideas here for the Adventurer in your life as well. Ships world-wide; express UK delivery.

'Make voyages! Attempt them! There's nothing else.'

TENNESSEE WILLIAMS

KIDS' CORNER

*W*hat do you buy for your kids? That's a really difficult question. The only thing you can know for sure is that you'll be spending a fortune on gifts and toys for many years to come. Most kids go through the dinosaurs stage, the Lego stage, the Barbie stage (depending on which sex they are, of course), the Transformers stage, the remote-controlled car stage – and did I omit the train set stage? (Some of them never grow out of it!) Stop reading here if you think you're going to get nervous, as it gets worse… the paintballing, large gadget and computer stages. Quite frankly, whatever your budget, you are likely to spend a horrendous amount of money on your kids.

The real problem these days is that one Barbie, one Transformers model or one Lego set is never enough. Once hooked, the kids want loads more (and the manufacturers encourage them all the way); they will bother and beg you every time you go near the shops, hoping you will eventually give in. I might sound weak-minded here, but by golly I have given in, many times, if I thought I'd get a few hours' peace and quiet. I defy any of you, honestly – and I mean honestly – to say that you never give in.

At ages 17, 19 and 21, my kids are now into the driving lessons, car and fancy clothes stages, which mean they have become even more expensive. These days I have to rely on sales assistants, rather than my kids, to tell me about the latest 'must-have' toys. There are so many places where you can buy gifts for kids that I've restricted the list here to my favourites. I hope you enjoy shopping from them.

Charlie Crow
www.charliecrow.com
This is an excellent place to find kids' dressing-up costumes: choose from animal, dinosaur, mythical or historical costumes, as well as outfits for Easter, Halloween and Christmas. Also on offer are dressing-up accessories, such as swords, masks and – to make you really popular with the parents – kids' make-up! Ships worldwide; express UK delivery.

The Dollshouse Emporium
www.dollshouse.com
If you're buying for a girl who loves dolls' houses, take a look at this wonderful emporium based in Ripley, Derbyshire. But be warned: you could end up spending a fortune. The website features fully decorated dolls' houses and thousands of colour-coordinated miniature room sets, plus carpets, flooring, lighting, wallpapers and more. Worldwide delivery.

Dude that's Cool Magic
www.dudethatscoolmagic. co.uk
You'll have to keep this book close to hand so that you can remember the name of this website! But this online store is worth remembering as it's bursting with magic tricks (close-up and otherwise), card tricks and street magic, plus props and illusions, for both the beginner and more experienced 'magician'. The website is colourful and includes an excellent section on children's magic shows. Ships worldwide; express UK delivery.

The Early Learning Centre
www.elc.co.uk
The baby and toddler section at the Early Learning Centre is well worth having a look around. You'll find a wide range of ideas that are perfect for your baby, including bath toys, Blossom Farm baby toys,

buggy and cot toys, and just about every other type of baby toy you can think of. The website is both clear and colourful. Express UK delivery.

The Great Little Trading Company
www.gltc.co.uk
Here is a great range of ideas for babies and young children, including sleeping bags, Fairy Ballerina and Sports Champion duvet sets and accessories, reasonably priced furniture (both themed and traditional), playtables and innovative storage ideas. Ships worldwide; express UK delivery.

Hamleys
www.hamleys.co.uk
If you've ever visited this world-famous Regent Street toy emporium (I hate the word, but it's the only way to describe this store), you'll know that it offers a huge range of toys, games, gadgets, puzzles and stocking fillers for all ages and in every price band. Worldwide delivery and gift wrapping.

Lambs Toys
www.lambstoys.co.uk
This is another of those toy retailers that offers so many brands it's hard to know where to begin. Let's start by saying that they have an excellent range of Meccano, Hornby and Scalextric, plus Lego, Schleich models, Power Rangers and Flashing Storm scooters, Zapf Baby Annabel, Chou Chou and Colette. Ships worldwide; express UK delivery.

Lingards Games
www.lingardsgames.co.uk
This website is definitely not just for children; it's for anyone who likes games (and jigsaw puzzles). Here you'll find old and new favourites, such as Monopoly and Labyrinth, World of Warcraft, Robo Rally, Murder Mystery and Casino Games. The range for younger children includes Junior Scrabble, Ludo and Halli Galli. There's loads to keep everyone quiet at Christmas and on rainy days. Ships worldwide; express UK delivery.

'Gifts, believe me, captivate both men and gods. Jupiter himself was won over and appeased by gifts.'

OVID

Mail Order Express
www.mailorderexpress.com

Mail Order Express claims to be the largest toy website in Europe, and who am I to argue? It's a hugely busy site with loads of offers and pre-order invitations on the home page, where, thankfully, you can shop by category – Music, Gadgets, Party, Science, Toy Vehicle, Dolls and Accessories – or by brand. Ships worldwide; express UK delivery.

Ollipops
www.ollipops.com

Definitely for the younger members of the family, but the collection of puppets on offer here is excellent. The characters range from long-sleeved puppets and finger puppets to dressed hedgehogs, moles, badgers and toads. You're unlikely to go very wrong here. Worldwide delivery.

The Toy Shop
www.thetoyshop.com

Now one of the largest independent toy retailers in the UK, the Toy Shop offers a huge range of choice, and has an excellent, easy-to-navigate website, where you can search by brand, type of toy, age group or price. The list of brands is phenomenal, and whatever you're looking for, you'll probably find it here. Ships worldwide; express UK delivery.

Toys by Mail Order
www.toysbymailorder.co.uk

Toys by Mail Order specialises in toys, gifts, games, nursery items and jigsaw puzzles for children of all ages. There is a lovely range of wooden and soft toys for baby and toddler gifts, numerous items for older boys and girls, plus traditional family games. They offer gift-wrapping and personalised messages for special occasions, plus fast delivery.

Toys Direct to Your Door
www.toysdirecttoyourdoor.co.uk

Some websites for toys are designed in such a frenetic style they make any self-respecting adult want to run away. Not this one. It is far more approachable than many, and you're immediately drawn in. You will find Playmobil, Thomas trains, Sylvanian Families, Lego and Duplo, Brio, Schleich animals and much more. Worldwide delivery.

3 GIFT ESSENTIALS

RIBBON AND WRAP

If you're anything like me, you spend a great deal of time picking the perfect present for someone only to discover that when you're ready, willing and able to hand it over you're missing the other vital component parts of ribbon, wrap and card. The easiest way to get round this is to keep a really good store of beautiful wrapping essentials, and to collect gorgeous/funny/silly cards when you find them. The sites listed in this section are all treasure troves of beautiful things, and it's all too easy to get carried away – don't say I didn't warn you.

See also Birthdays, page 18.

Carnmeal Cottage
www.carnmeal.co.uk
This site is a must for anyone has always has lots of gifts to wrap and appreciates the value of presentation. It offers a wide choice of beautiful ribbons and craft accessories for all occasions. Choose from wired and unwired ribbons, organza and tartans, all of them in lots of different widths and a wide selection of colours. World-wide delivery.

Jaycotts
www.jaycotts.co.uk
The haberdashery and ribbon departments on this site offer double-faced satin, taffeta, tartan, gold-edged satin and gold and silver lamé, all sold by the metre. Ships worldwide; orders over £25 delivered free.

National Trust Shop
www.nationaltrust-shop. co.uk
The National Trust online shop always has one of the best ranges of high-quality wrapping paper and gift tags at Christmas. Apart from stocking a wide choice of designs, it also sells wrap in different lengths up to 20 metres. UK delivery usually within five working days.

Orchard Cards

www.orchardcards.co.uk

Orchard cards not only offer a wide selection of high-quality cards for all types of occasion and a reminder calendar into which you can put all your important dates, but they also sell extremely attractive wrapping paper. Free delivery for orders of ten or more items.

The Ribbon Shop

www.theribbonshop.co.uk

There are wonderful ribbons here for all occasions (including Christmas), and what's different is that they're all beautifully photographed and decoratively wrapped around parcels, hat boxes, candles and treats. Prices are reasonable and they'll deliver worldwide.

VV Rouleaux

www.vvrouleaux.com

The famous ribbon and trimmings emporium based in Marylebone Lane, London, is now online. Here you can choose from a delightful range of grosgrain, organdie, wire-edged, velvet and gingham ribbons, as well as beaded strands, feathers and much more. Worldwide delivery.

WRAP IT UP

- In the USA 4 million tons of gift wrap and shopping bags are thrown away after the winter holidays.
- In China, red gift wrap connotes luck.
- In Japan cloth gift wrap, called *furoshiki,* is very popular.
- In Korea traditional gift wrapping cloths are called *bojagi*.

CHOCOLATES

Chocolates make great gifts for lots of occasions, though giving them for birthdays and as Christmas presents might make it seem as if you've really run out of ideas. They're useful as stocking fillers or thank-you gifts, certainly; but as the main present? I think not. They're wonderful to take with you when you're a guest, to send as a thank you, or to add as an extra 'something' at any time. There are now so many places to shop for chocolates that it's best to use your budget to buy something small, delicious, beautifully packaged and with an air of exclusivity. Choose from one of the following and you'll be popular all round.

See also Valentine's Day, page 28.

Brownes
www.brownes.co.uk
Brownes offer luxurious handmade chocolates in four sizes of box, ranging from a small selection to their 1-kg presentation box. They include after-dinner mint 'chasers', buttered Brazil nuts, dusted almonds and chocolate-covered raisins. They all look totally delicious, and once seen, you'll certainly want to try. Delivers worldwide

Chococo
www.chococo.co.uk
Alongside the celebration hampers and chunky chocolates on offer here you'll find other goodies, such as Chilli Tickles and Raspberry Riots. Chococo always have excellent ideas for Easter, including giant goodie boxes, chocolate hens and wonderfully colourful eggs for both adults and children. Ships to EU and UK; gift wrapping and express UK delivery.

Cocoa Loco
www.cocoaloco.co.uk
This company's organic chocolates are hand-made using high-quality ingredients. Try treats such as Dark Chocolate-covered Ginger; Mango, Orange and Hazelnut Milk Chocolate Truffles; the Hot and Spicy Special (with Chocolate Chilli

Brownies) or Jumbo Chocolate Buttons. Ships worldwide; express UK delivery.

Dark Sugars

www.darksugars.co.uk

Hand-made chocolate truffles, with enticing flavours such as apricot and brandy, cardamom and orange, and dry apple cider and cinnamon, are on offer from Dark Sugars. They also offer chocolate-dipped, liqueur-soaked dried fruits, such as prunes in Armagnac, cherries in cherry brandy and peaches in schnapps. Yum! Worldwide delivery.

Green & Blacks

www.greenandblacksdirect.com

Now a household name, this company is a must for beautifully packaged, high-quality organic chocolate at a reasonable price. You can order selections of their chocolate bars, tied with ribbon; gift boxes such as The Chocolate Gardener and Coffee Indulgence; or use their bespoke service to create your own selection. UK delivery.

Leonidas

www.leonidasbelgianchocolates.co.uk

For the ultimate in Belgian chocolates visit Leonidas – in person at Selfridges or Harrods, or on this dedicated website, and make your choice from the chocolate menu. Choose from possibilities such as Butter Creams, the General Assortment, milk or dark chocolates, Neapolitans and Liqueurs. UK delivery; express available.

Montezuma's

www.montezumas.co.uk

Montezuma's produces a range of around forty different hand-made truffles, with names such as Caribbean Rhythm, Irish Tipple and Lost in Space. You can order one of their luscious ready-made collections, or create your own from their menu. You can also buy organic drinking chocolate, fantastic fudge and chocolate hampers here. Ships worldwide; express UK delivery.

FLOWERS

Nothing says it quite like flowers. From the smallest posy to the biggest bouquet, fabulous florals are always welcome.

See also Valentine's Day, page 28.

Designer Flowers
www.designerflowers.org.uk

The florists at Designer Flowers create all their own arrangements for every type of occasion, and they are delivered direct by courier, in secure boxes, to London and across the UK. You can include champagne, Belgian chocolates, balloons and soft toys in your gift. Apart from fresh bouquets, they also offer silk arrangements. Express UK delivery.

Flowerworks
www.flowerworksoxford.co.uk

Flowerworks provide a selection of their favourite seasonal bouquets, and also offer a facility for you to design your own. To do this, just answer their questions on style and arrangement, provide information on colour choice, price and the recipient, then leave the rest to them. Express UK delivery.

Lambert's Flowers
www.lambertsflowercompany.co.uk

On this stylish website, Lambert's offer a small but cleverly designed collection of bouquets and arrangements. There are gorgeous new baby gifts on offer, special flowers for Valentine's Day and other occasions, plus teddies, chocolates and vases. Express UK delivery.

World of Roses
www.worldofroses.com

This is the place to find outstanding roses, from climbers and floribundas to ground cover and hybrid tea varieties. However, don't expect to find your standard hand-tied bunches here; this company specialises in gorgeous roses for planting in the garden – a beautifully enduring gift. You can order them in pots, bare-rooted or gift wrapped, and simply select the date that you want them delivered. Express UK delivery.

THE PERFUMERY

Fragrance is one of the most popular gifts because it's easy to buy, simple to wrap and straightforward to send. It's also all too easy to get wrong. If you know, or can find out, a person's favourite fragrance, you can go down the beautifully packaged lotion and potion route without any problems. Otherwise you need to be extremely careful. Don't buy something for someone else just because *you* love it. Choose according to the recipient's style and personality, and leave yourself totally out of the mix. If you're in doubt but really want to give a pampering present, I suggest you go for a high-quality scented candle, such as Essence of John Galliano by Diptyque, Orange Blossom by Jo Malone or Blue Tangerine by Kenneth Turner. You'll be happily thanked whichever you buy.

Escentual

www.escentual.co.uk

Escentual carry possibly the widest range of fragrances for men and women in the UK. Whatever you're searching for, be it perfume or related bath and body product, you're almost certain to find it here. Brands include Burberry, Bulgari, Calvin Klein, Gucci, Guerlain, Crabtree & Evelyn, Rochas, Versace, Tisserand and I Coloniali. Delivery in the UK is free on orders over £30; the company also offers free gift wrapping.

Floris London

www.florislondon.com

Established since 1730, Floris is one of the oldest and most traditional perfumers. Perennial favourites on offer include Lavender, China Rose, Gardenia and Stephanotis; while popular modern fragrances include Night-Scented Jasmine, Bouquet de la Reine and No 89. Each fragrance has a full range of bath and body products to accompany it. There are also special wrapped sets for Christmas. Ships worldwide; express UK option.

Garden Pharmacy
www.garden.co.uk

Here you'll find well-known brands such as Chanel, Revlon, Elizabeth Arden, Lancôme, Clinique and Clarins, together with Vichy, Avene, Caudalie and Roc, and spa products by I Coloniali, L'Occitane, Roger et Gallet and Segreti Mediterranei (and no doubt a few more will have appeared by the time you read this). The range of fragrances on offer is huge as well. They also offer free gift wrapping and 24-hour delivery.

Kiarie
www.kiarie.co.uk

Online home fragrance retailer Kiarie has one of the best ranges of scented candles available, including brands such as Geodosis, Kenneth Turner, Manuel Canovas, Creation Mathias, Rigaud and Millefiori. There are literally hundreds to choose from at all price levels. Ships worldwide; express UK delivery and gift wrapping.

L'Artisan Parfumeur
www.laboutiquedelartisan-parfumeur.com

If you're not already aware of this gorgeous collection of French fragrance and bath and body products, now's the time to discover them. With names such as Mure et Musc, Figuier and Orchidée Blanche, this is a beautifully presented range. Buy from their pretty London store or online. Ships worldwide; express UK delivery plus gift wrapping.

Les Senteurs
www.lessenteurs.com

Les Senteurs is a famous perfumery based in London, offering different and unusual fragrances with related bath and body products. Brands on offer include Creed, Annick Goutal, Diptyque, E. Coudray, Serge Lutens, Carons and Parfums Historique to name but a few. Worldwide delivery and gift wrapping.

L'Occitane
www.loccitane.com

With stores now located around the world, L'Occitane is well known and deservedly so. Its range includes fragrances, body, hand and hair care, bath and shower products, and home fragrances. Among the scents are Lavender, Oranger, Verbena Harvest, Eau d'Ambre and Green Tea to name just a few. Ships worldwide; express UK delivery plus a gift wrapping service.

Miller Harris

www.millerharris.com

This is a small, independent company with outlets in capital cities worldwide. It specialises in blending its own fragrances, which have enticing names such as Tangerine Vert, Fleur Oriental and Terre de Bois. Each range includes the eau de parfum, plus bath and body products, and candles. Ships worldwide; express UK delivery and gift wrapping.

Natural Magic

www.naturalmagicuk.com

Natural Magic candles are around twice the size and weight of an average candle, being about 1 kg each. They have three wicks and up to seventy-five hours of burn time. Every candle is scented for a specific purpose, such as uplifting, inspiring, soothing and destressing; all are beautifully packaged, and perfect for treats and gifts. Ships worldwide; express UK delivery.

Ormonde Jayne

www.ormondejayne.com

This is a gorgeous, luxurious perfumery, and whether you manage to visit the boutique in the Royal Arcade off London's Bond Street, or buy from the

'Perfume puts the finishing touch to elegance – a detail that subtly underscores the look, an invisible extra that completes a woman's personality. Without it there is something missing.'

GIANNI VERSACE

online store, you can be confident of investing in something really special. Fragrances have names such as Osmanthus, Champaca, Frangipani and Orris Noir. Ships worldwide; express UK delivery plus gift wrapping

Penhaligons

www.penhaligons.co.uk

Penhaligons, an old English firm, now have an international reputation. They offer fragrances, candles and bath and body products which make perfect and luxurious gifts. Choose from classics such as Lily of the Valley, Elizabethan Rose or Bluebell; or more modern and spicy scents, such as Malabah, Artemesia or LP No 9. Each fragrance is matched to a shower gel, soap, body lotion and candle. Gift-wrapping is gorgeous and free, and they deliver worldwide.

PERFECT PAMPERING

What is 'pampering' exactly? The dictionary describes it as being indulged, spoilt or cared for, and that's certainly the kind of pampering that I like. To my mind, it includes anything from buying yourself a gorgeous new lipstick on a dull day to having a massage on a remote island surrounded by blue sea and golden sands, and with the breeze blowing through your hair. (I offer no apologies for the clichés!)

I asked other people how they would describe pampering and they came up with the suggestions opposite. From that list you can see that it relates to anything relaxing, enjoyable and therapeutic. It includes shopping (of course), champagne, lying in the bath surrounded by candles (whether you've lit them or someone else has); beauty products and treatments. So go on, pamper someone today – the choice of how you do so is all yours.

BATHTIME PAMPERING
Bath & Unwind
www.bathandunwind.com
Bath & Unwind specialises in luxury products that help you to relax after a hard day's work (or play). Aromatherapy Associates, Burt's Bees, Calmia, Korres, Mother Earth, Nougat and Jane Packer are just some of the brands on offer. Ships worldwide; express UK delivery.

Simply Roses
www.simplyroses.com
There are perfect gifts here for anyone who loves roses. Among the exclusive collection of luxurious, rose-inspired products are bath oil, perfumed pomanders, candles and pretty soaps, Savon de Marseilles and bath truffles. Worldwide delivery and gift packaging.

'Youth is unduly busy with pampering the outer person.'
HORACE

Ideal pampering

'A really amazing massage during a holiday is the ultimate way to unwind.'

'Spending the day sunbathing and then horse riding on the beach is about as close to the perfect day as I can get.'

'Having time to myself, with no distractions; or a pile of glossy, undemanding magazines that I can devour.'

'Having a stylist making you beautiful.'

'Getting home from work to find flowers on the table, dinner cooked and a candlelit bubble bath waiting.'

'A visit to the hairdresser for a new style; a surprise weekend away; the treat of a new outfit.'

'A new book and a pair of cashmere socks.'

'A glass of wine in front of an open fire in a holiday cottage.'

'An Indian head massage.'

'A full day at a spa to include a massage, a special bath, a facial, a steam treatment, and a manicure/pedicure.'

'Caviar and champagne – as much as you can handle!'

'Sunset at the beach with champagne followed by dinner.'

'A full day of shopping and no questions asked about how much you spent when you return with a car full of packages!'

'A cruise on a luxurious private yacht with twelve staff to service your every need.'

'Pampering means lying on the sofa on a mid-week afternoon with a good book in one hand and a cup of tea in the other, magically provided by my husband .

SPA SOLO (OR MAYBE NOT)

Bliss London

www.blisslondon.co.uk

Sign up for Bliss Beut e-mails and stay 'in the glow'. Does that give you some idea of the tone of New York and London's hottest spa? You can give someone a voucher to visit the spa, or a selection of their products, with names such Body Butter, Rosy Toes and Glamour Glove Gel. Ships worldwide; express UK delivery.

Cowshed

www.cowshedonline.com

This company is recognised for its fun, bovine-inspired names, such as Dirty Cow Hand Wash, Until the Cows Come Home Gift Set, and Grumpy Cow uplifting candle (so you really do need to know the person you're giving them to). Cowshed products are high quality and attractively packaged. UK and US delivery.

OOH LA LA COLOUR

Becca

www.beccacosmetics.com

This is a modern cosmetics brand that offers unique products, such as their Brazilian bronzing sheen, Best of Becca palette and 'Ultimate' mascara. The products make terrific presents for make-up addicts like me. Ships worldwide; express UK delivery.

Benefit

www.benefitcosmetics. co.uk

Benefit are always introducing new and clever ideas, most of which make excellent girly gifts that you barely need to wrap, including special little gift sets at Christmas. Ships worldwide; express UK delivery and gift wrapping.

Bobbi Brown

www.bobbibrown.co.uk

This is the perfect gift store for contemporary cosmetics lovers. Anything here is 'gift worthy'. They launch new products and sets on a regular basis, some of which are limited editions, so keep your eyes open and snap them up. UK delivery via this website.

Boots

www.boots.com

The Boots stores are unlikely to carry the full extent of the range that is available online: Chanel, Clarins, Clinique, Dior, Estée Lauder, Elizabeth Arden and Lancôme, plus ultra-modern brands Ruby & Millie, Urban Decay and Benefit. Delivery is free when you spend £40, and returns are free. Express delivery.

Eyes Lips Face

www.eyeslipsface.co.uk

This beauty brand is hot in the USA, and has just launched its website in the UK. Their line of simple, luxurious, problem-solving and extremely well-priced cosmetics and accessories are commonly priced at £1.50 or less (excluding kits). At this price, you can afford to play. UK delivery.

MAC

www.maccosmetics.co.uk

You've seen their cosmetics in all the best beauty stores: now you can buy them online, direct from their ultra-chic website. Shop by category – lips, eyes, nails, skincare and so forth – or from one of their collections, with names such as Viva Glam, Barbie Loves Mac, Untamed, Rockocco or Technacolour. UK delivery; express option.

NARS

www.narscosmetics.co.uk

This is one of my favourite websites, and I must seriously try resist buying too frequently. Buy someone their 'Orgasm' blush, one of the best colours you can find anywhere, and you'll be extremely popular. There's lots more on offer as well. UK delivery from this site; express delivery from www. SpaceNK.co.uk. Products also available from Liberty of London and House of Fraser.

Pixi

www.pixibeauty.com

'Magical, individual, feminine, small, playful, free-spirited, mischievous, friendly, colourful, cheeky, unique, illusive, cute, and tempting' are the words the founders of this London-based company use to describe their 'wake-up make-up'. They offer well-priced beauty kits, scents and lots of gift ideas to choose from too. Look at the favourites page for some personal recommendations. Worldwide delivery.

NATURAL EXPERTS

Espa

www.espaonline.com

This is a light and modern website offering Espa's famous range of aromatherapy products, from specific beauty treatments to bath and body products and luxury gifts. Everything is formulated from the highest-quality, organically grown plants. Worldwide delivery.

Liz Earle

www.lizearle.com

Liz Earle has a beautiful website offering her 'Naturally Active Skincare' – a pampering range of skin, body and suncare products. Shimmers for body and lips, Vital Aromatherapy Oils and travel mini-kits from the wide range are just some of the temptations on offer, and the lovely packaging is an extra bonus. Ships worldwide; express UK delivery.

Mandala Aroma

www.mandala-aroma.com

Mandala Aroma is a luxury organic aromatherapy company set up by ex-fashion buyer and qualified aromatherapist Gillian Kavanagh. Here you'll discover bath oils, body treatment oils and candles all under the headings of Wisdom, Love, Courage and Strength. Worldwide delivery.

SO WHAT'S NEW?

Women have been using pampering potions on themselves at least as far back as the ancient Egyptians, if not before. Legend tells us that Cleopatra bathed in asses' milk to preserve the beauty that enthralled Julius Caesar and Marc Antony. And excavations on Tutankhamun's tomb (from an era over a thousand years earlier) uncovered cosmetics jars containing traces of 3000-year-old skin cream, created from nine parts animal fat to one part perfume resin.

Must Have

www.musthave.co.uk

Must Have, based in Leamington Spa, offer natural and organic skincare products, bodycare, fragrance and cosmetics from around the world. You'll find REN, Paul & Joe, Anthony Logistics, Cowshed, Jo Wood Organics, Headonism Organic Haircare, Living Nature and Abahna alongside brands you probably already know, such as Nailtiques, Phyto and Caudalie. Ships worldwide; express UK delivery plus gift wrapping.

Mysa Natural

www.mysanatural.com

Essential elements of natural ingredients and must-have treats meet beautifully here. Think Pink Grapefruit Hand and Body Lotion, Ginger Loofah Soap or Sweet Jasmine Body Scrub and you'll get the idea.

Neal's Yard Remedies

www.nealsyardremedies. com

The shop takes its name from Neal's Yard in Covent Garden, where it was first established. Since then, Neal's Yard Remedies has grown into one of the country's leading natural product retailers. The website offers luxurious bath and bodycare products, aromatherapy, herbal, homeopathic and flower remedies, as well as attractively packaged gift sets. Ships worldwide; express UK delivery.

Origins

www.origins.co.uk

Origins are experts in natural skincare. You'll find them in large department stores, as well as online. Products such as their luxurious Ginger Soufflé Whipped Body Cream, Jump Start Body Wash and Pomegranate Wash cleanser will leave you yearning to try them all. See if you can bear to give them away. Express UK delivery.

Potions and Possibilities

www.potions.co.uk

Natural toiletries and aromatherapy products, ranging from soaps and bath oils to restorative balms and creams, are all available online. Choose from bath sizzlers, shower gels, shampoos, massage oils, body balms, fragrances and gift collections, including gorgeously wrapped soaps. Ships worldwide; express UK delivery.

> '**To do nothing is sometimes a good remedy.**'
>
> HIPPOCRATES

Puresha

www.puresha.com

This is an attractive place to shop, with lovely photographs of luxurious natural beauty products you're bound to want to buy, such as Patyka, Ginger & Smart, Chocolate Sun, Hamadi and Perfect Organics, plus REN, l'Artisan Parfumeur and Mama Mio. Ships to UK, Ireland, Australia and the USA. Express UK delivery and gift wrapping.

Rose Apothecary

www.rose-apothecary. co.uk

Here's a company website with a difference, as it offers lots of their own prettily packaged products, such as Rose Petal Bath and Shower Creme, Lavender Shampoo and luxurious gift boxes, as well as hard-to-find brands. Worldwide delivery.

Urban Apothecary

www.urbanapothecary. co.uk

Whether you're looking for a pampering gift or something for yourself, you'll almost certainly like this website, which is easy to use and well photographed. Categories include Beauty, Skincare, Home Fragrance, Candles, and Gifts & Accessories from brands such as Korres, Sohum and This Works. UK delivery; express option plus gift wrapping.

SKIN DEEP

The beauty brands below produce superb products and give great service on their websites. Most offer express delivery and gift wrapping.

Clinique
www.clinique.co.uk

Crème de la Mer
www.cremedelamer.co.uk

Estée Lauder
www.esteelauder.co.uk

Lancôme
www.lancome.co.uk

FABULOUS FASHION

Fashion is not necessarily the first thing you will think of when wondering what to buy as a gift, and I'm certainly not suggesting that Miu Miu handbags, Jimmy Choo shoes or vintage Hervé Léger dresses are essential for your shopping list at pressie-choosing time. If they *are*, the person you're buying for is very lucky – and please don't leave me out! If you're thinking of something a little bit less amazing, consider of-the-moment belts, bangles and 'bling' (I know, but I couldn't think of anything else beginning with 'b') that you'll find alongside all the major pieces at the best fashion stores. These stores are always worth browsing in for ideas for fashion-conscious friends. You really don't have to spend a fortune, and you'll probably find something wonderful that she would never have thought of herself.

Here are some of my favourites; you'll find more in Fashion Victim, page 134.

Black
www.black.co.uk
Here you'll find gorgeous and not overpriced shawls and scarves, gloves, bags, jewels and belts in neutrals, such as black, grey, cream and beige. Ships worldwide; express UK delivery and gift wrapping.

Brora
www.brora.co.uk
Founded with the aim of giving traditional cashmere a new, contemporary look, Brora sells some lovely things. Cashmere gloves, wristwarmers, hats and stoles are just a few of the gift ideas you can find here; it all

'Fashion fades, only style remains the same.'
COCO CHANEL

Burberry is an internationally renowned brand with a history that dates back to 1870. Thomas Burberry was a draper whose designs became popular with the royal family. The company developed the first gabardine raincoat in 1880: it was breathable, weatherproof and tearproof. They also developed the trenchcoats worn in the Boer War and the First World War.

depends on how much you want to spend. Cashmere, in just about any form, always makes a wonderful gift. The collection extends to men, children and babies. Brora cashmere is dyed and knitted in a mill in Hawick, Scotland, and uses the waters of the local River Teviot. Ships worldwide; express UK delivery and gift wrapping.

Browns Fashion
www.brownsfashion.com
The Browns stores are on South Molton Street and Sloane Street in London. Their website offers a mouthwatering list of contemporary designers, including Lanvin, Balenciaga, Missoni and Paul Smith plus Dolce & Gabbana, Roberto Cavalli, Ann Demeulemeester and Issa. For gifts, take a look first at the accessories section. Ships worldwide; express UK delivery and gift wrapping.

Burberry
www.burberry.com
Browse the luxuriously photographed collections, including Burberry Prorsum, Burberry London and the Icons Collection, then go to Shop Online and choose from menswear, womenswear, bags and accessories. Ships to most EU countries; US orders must go through burberry.com. Express UK delivery and gift wrapping.

Celtic Sheepskin
www.celtic-sheepskin.co.uk
There are some excellent clothes and accessories here, particularly for the winter months, including everything from excellent quality, full-length shearling coats and chic Toscana gilets to gloves and scarves, sheepskin-lined boots and slippers, waistcoats and cute shearling duffels, and boots for children. Delivers throughout the UK.

Ewenique
www.ewenique.co.uk
This is a very attractive and comprehensive range of leather, suede and shearling coats and jackets for men and women. They offer various styles of flying jacket, and accessories such as scarves, stoles, hats, hide bags, gloves and snuggly slippers. Worldwide delivery.

Jaeger
www.jaeger.co.uk
Jaeger has been a luxury brand for over 120 years. They have recently relaunched their updated accessories collection and it's really good. Reasonably priced but up-to-the-moment handbags and modern jewels are just part of what's on offer. Express UK delivery and gift wrapping.

Karen Millen
www.karenmillen.co.uk
Here you'll find modern bags at reasonable prices, excellent knitwear and contemporary jackets and coats. Having recently bought a black leather biker jacket here for my daughter, I can tell you it was a great success, so check here for fashionable gifts for the fashion conscious aged 17-plus. UK delivery; express option.

Paul Smith
www.paulsmith.co.uk
Paul Smith is a designer respected around the world for his quintessential 'Englishness'. On his website you'll find a selection of jeans, shoes, knitwear, T-shirts and accessories, plus a small amount of tailoring. This is a great place for gifts for Paul Smith fans. Ships worldwide; express UK delivery and gift wrapping.

Peruvian Connection
www.peruvianconnection. co.uk
Peruvian Connection was founded in 1976, almost by accident, when mother and daughter team Biddie and Annie Harlbut fell in love with the crafts and designs they discovered in Peru. For gifts, go straight to the jewellery section, where you'll find a really creative range of pretty beaded earrings and necklaces. There are also unique scarves and bags. Ships worldwide; express UK delivery and gift wrapping.

Pure Collection
www.purecollection.com
There's a really good collection of high-quality cashmere here, but I would stick to the

pashmina scarves and shawls for gifts. No, don't say they're out of fashion; find me someone who doesn't love to wear them. Buy something in the latest season's hot colour and you'll be considered a star. Ships worldwide; express UK delivery and gift wrapping.

Red Direct
www.reddirect.co.uk
What started as a small off-shoot of *Red* magazine has now become a treasure trove of cleverly chosen jewellery, watches, handbags, shoes, belts and pretty leather accessories by designers such as CC Skye, Rebecca Lau, Belen Echandia, Osprey and Ollie & Nic. Ships worldwide; express UK delivery.

Sundance Catalog
www.sundancecatalog.com
Inspired (and initiated) by the actor Robert Redford, Sundance grew out of the success of the General Store in his Sundance Village. It is a truly American catalogue that has now become a worldwide on-line store. You'll discover wonderful jewellery by American craftsmen, ranch-style boots, home accessories (gorgeous quilts and throws) and lots of other ideas for gifts. Worldwide delivery and gift wrapping.

Toast
www.toastbypost.co.uk
You need to be slightly careful here to make sure that you're buying for a 'Toast' person and not a total fashion victim, but the company offers lovely and interesting scarves and jewels that you won't find anywhere else. Ships worldwide; express UK delivery and gift wrapping.

Whistles
www.whistles.co.uk
Whistles is a really clever and fun place to shop. There are separates, day and evening dresses, outerwear and accessories, all in their own idiosyncratic contemporary style. Their pretty tops and cardis in the latest colours are especially good for gifts. They deliver to the UK and Ireland; express option in UK.

Did you know?
Browns founder, Joan Burstein, is credited with discovering contemporary fashion talents such as John Galliano, Alexander McQueen, Hussein Chalayan and Commes des Garcons.

LUSCIOUS LINGERIE

Perhaps you think lingerie stores sell only lacy nothings in gorgeous colours. In fact, they also have some really lovely gift ideas, particularly for older teen daughters like mine. Look for tights in the latest colours, or print, lace and fishnet versions; cut-off leggings with lace trim (often available in a rainbow of colours); legwarmers (cashmere, if you can stretch to it); and really pretty camisoles and tops.

See also 'Wisps of Lace' in Valentine's Day, page 37.

Figleaves
www.figleaves.com
Whichever brand, size or colour of lingerie, swimwear or nightwear you need, you'll probably find it here. The labels include DKNY, Dolce & Gabbana, Janet Reger, Sloggi, Gossard and Wonderbra. Their fitting guidelines are excellent. Delivery is free to anywhere the world. Express delivery and gift wrapping are optional extras.

My Tights
www.mytights.co.uk
My Tights have a really modern and easy-to-use website, offering a range of hosiery brands, including Aristoc, Charnos, Elbeo, Gerbe, La Perla, Levante and Pretty Polly, to name but a few. Ships worldwide; express UK delivery.

Tights Please
www.tightsplease.co.uk
Whether you want fishnets, crochet tights, bright colours, knee-highs, stay-ups, stockings or footsies, you'll find them all here, together with legwarmers, socks, and maternity and bridal hosiery. Worldwide express delivery.

Wolford London
www.wolfordboutique london.com
Wolford pledge to make you look good, and their superb hosiery, body shapewear, tops and lingerie should certainly do the trick. You can now purchase their collection online through their London shop in South Molton Street. They ship worldwide and offer express UK delivery.

CHAMPAGNE AND WINE

You might think that giving wine and champagne as a gift is just that little bit too easy, but consider it for a moment. When have you ever been disappointed by receiving a bottle of bubbly? I certainly haven't.

Some of the websites here offer the facility of personalising the bottle label, or of ordering jeroboams, methuselahs and nebuchadnezzars of champagne (and no, I'm not going to tell you, you'll find out below). These would make wonderful gifts for special occasions, such as silver wedding anniversaries and special birthdays. On other sites you'll find really high-quality selections of wines where you can just take your pick or take their advice. If you know that someone likes a particular wine, you could use www.wine-searcher.com to track it down. Before you shell out for that bottle of Pomerol, just bear in mind that the prices you'll find there do not include VAT.

Balls Brothers
www.ballsbrothers.co.uk

Balls Brothers has shipped and traded wines for over 150 years, so you can be confident that they have a prime selection. They offer a hand-picked range of over 400 wines, and you can be sure that everything has been carefully chosen, from the least expensive (reds start at around £4.50 a bottle) right up to the pricey Chateau Palmer Margaux (at over £100). UK delivery.

Berry Brothers & Rudd
www.bbr.com

Berry Bros. & Rudd (BBR) is Britain's oldest wine and spirit merchant, having traded from the same shop in St James's for over 300 years. You can find out not only about the wines you should be drinking now, but also about how to start a BBR Cellar Plan, use their Wedding List services and join their Wine Club. Ships worldwide; express UK delivery.

Butlers Wines

www.butlerswines.co.uk

Butlers sell high-quality wine and champagne gifts at very reasonable prices. You can assemble your own gift. by choosing from the wines listed and perhaps including hand-made truffles. They offer a good choice of hampers as well. Express UK delivery.

Cambridge Wine

www.cambridgewine.com

This is a beautifully designed website from a Cambridge-based independent wine merchant, and one that's a pleasure to browse. Choose by category and by country; select from their mixed cases and promotional offers; and take advantages of their gift and *en primeur* services. UK delivery.

Champagne Warehouse

www.champagneware-house.co.uk

Here is an attractive website from a retailer established just a few years ago. It offers personally selected, top-quality champagnes that you can purchase by the bottle, or in cases of six or twelve. Prices start at around £14.00 per bottle. UK delivery.

Jeroboams

www.jeroboams.co.uk

This is a beautifully photographed website from a luxury wine and food specialist. They offer inviting gifts of food and wine, such as port with Stilton; vodka and caviar; or whisky and Cheddar. Choose one of their luxury hampers, or from their list of wines, champagnes and spirits. UK delivery.

Just Champagne

www.justchampagne.co.uk

This retailer offers not 'just' champagne but also gifts, such as champagne truffles, picnic bags, teddies and sterling silver cufflinks. As well as a range of single bottles and magnums (two bottles), you will find generous jeroboams (3 litres), hefty methuselahs (6 litres) and gigantic nebuchadnezzars (15 litres). That last one is definitely mine – want to share? EU and express UK delivery.

Laithwaites

www.laithwaites.co.uk

This family-run wine merchant offers a personal and efficient service, and a very good choice of wines and champagnes in all price ranges. They also have a wide range of fortified wines and spirits. and there's even a

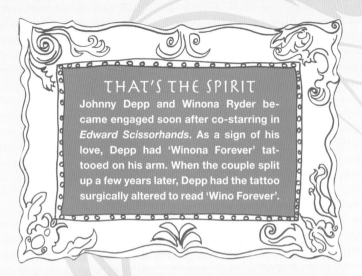

clever food-matching service. UK delivery.

Lay & Wheeler
www.laywheeler.co.uk
This company has been owned and run by the Wheeler family for six generations. Specialising in Bordeaux and Burgundies, Lay & Wheeler are also agents for wine producers in Australia, California, South Africa and other areas. There's wide range of wine on offer on this busy website, plus assistance if you need it. UK delivery.

Lords Wines
www.lordswines.co.uk
There's a good selection of food and wine gifts here, from beautifully packaged bottles of wine and champagne to more traditional combinations, such as port and Stilton, and champagne and chocolates. There are also excellent hampers, particularly a Christmas. Most gifts can be personalised – not just the card, but the box and wine label as well. Express UK delivery and gift wrapping.

Next Day Champagne
www.nextday-champagne. co.uk
Next day-champagne is a mail-order company that specialises in sending out personalised bottles of champagne. You can choose from a wide range

of champagnes that they will send out with your message, together with everything from a teddy bear to a Christmas pudding. You can also choose from their Lanson vintage selection and design your own personalised label. Express UK delivery.

The Drink Shop
www.thedrinkshop.com
This site offers a wide choice of champagnes, wines and spirits, cocktail kits for different types of drinks, gift hampers, presentation boxes, books and a selection of unusual luxury chocolates by Belgian retailers Gudrun and Lassiter, so if the booze enthusiast you're buying for also has a sweet tooth, you can buy everything together. EU and express delivery.

The Whisky Exchange
www.thewhiskyexchange. com
Although you can buy blended and some single malt whiskies from just about every supermarket and wine merchant, if you want a really good selection of whiskies, you need to have a look here. The list of single malts at The Whisky Exchange is amazing, and prices

go up to over £2000 (don't faint!). But of course there are plenty between £20 and £25 too. Ships worldwide; express UK delivery.

Wine Dancer
www.winedancer.com
Send a bottle of Veuve Clicquot in its very own ice bucket with your personalised card; or a boxed mini-bottle of Laurent Perrier with a candle and bath essence; or if you want to be really popular, send a methuselah of champagne (the equivalent of eight bottles) in a wooden crate. Cross your fingers that you'll be invited to share it. Ships worldwide; express UK delivery.

The Wooden Wine Box Company
www.woodenwinebox.co.uk
Take a look through this well-photographed online store for wine and champagne gifts. For once, there are no 'add on' teddies, chocolates or flowers – just high-quality, hand-picked wines and champagnes. All the bottles are packed in attractive pine gift boxes and can be sent out with your personal message. Delivery throughout the UK and to EU business addresses.

HAMPERS AND FOOD GIFTS

There's no doubt that the internet has completely changed the way we give gifts of food. Now you can easily order smoked salmon from the north of Scotland and have it sent to a friend who lives in Cornwall, or select a box filled with bottles of the highest-quality olive oil, Parma ham and vine tomatoes, or a basket full of fruit and flapjacks and have them delivered the following day. Best of all, at Christmas you can send wonderful marrons glacés, spiced nuts and Turkish delight and never even leave home. Bliss!

Bayley & Sage
www.bayley-sage.co.uk
Bayley & Sage is a top-quality delicatessen based in Wimbledon, London. On the website you can buy one of their well-composed gift selections, such as Sweet Sensation (jelly beans, chocolate brownies, mini cakes and marshmallows) or Gentleman's Selection (wine, coffee, marmalade, nuts and Gentlemen's Relish). UK delivery.

Claire MacDonald
www.claire-macdonald.com
Claire Macdonald's name is synonymous with excellent food and highland hospitality. She is married to Lord Macdonald, High Chief of Clan Macdonald, whose family have run Kinloch Lodge on the Isle of Skye as a luxury hotel for over three decades. Her website offers gifts of food and wine, such as The Chocolate Pudding Collection, Savoury Sauces and Chocolate Fudge, all beautifully packaged in signature dark green gift boxes. Buy from her (and visit her hotel as well if you can). She delivers worldwide.

London Fine Foods
www.efoodies.co.uk
This is an extremely tempting online food retailer, where you can order the highest-quality olive oil and balsamic vinegar, British and French cheeses, caviar, foie gras, black and white truffles, truffle oil, spices, mushrooms and

champagne. They also offer gift vouchers and an express delivery option.

Gogo Fruit Baskets
www.gogofruitbasket.com

Here you can buy fruit baskets and all sorts of 'hampers', including 'Pink Fizz, Strawberries and Chocs', 'Cheese and Wine', 'Mighty Fruit 'n' Muffin' and 'Big Fat Thank You' (the last contains muffins, caramel slices, macaroons, flapjack bars, caramelts and cupcakes). Express UK delivery.

Gorgeous Food
www.gorgeous-food.co.uk

Gorgeous by name and by nature, this selection of hampers has enticing names, such as 'Decadence', 'Luxury' and 'Indulgence', and includes themed selections, such as 'Afternoon Tea', 'Chocoholic', 'Spanish' and 'Chilli Lover'. The website displays not only the filled hamper, but also each ingredient on the list of what's included. Express UK delivery and gift wrapping.

Lakeland
www.lakelandlimited.co.uk

This family-run firm provides hundreds of excellent and original gift ideas. Its foodie treats include chocolates, Bay Tree Turkish Delight, Apricots in moscato, candied fruits, marrons glacés, olive oils, jalapeño spiced nuts and the famous Australian Celebration Cake. There's always a superb selection. Ships worldwide; express UK delivery. *See also Kitchen Genius, page 156.*

Lewis & Cooper
www.lewisandcooper.com

Lewis & Cooper offer a selection of hampers for all tastes and pockets. You can buy one of their ready-made hampers, or pick the items that you want included. Their wide range of foodstuffs extends from local

Mr Lewis and Mr Cooper first opened their Yorkshire-based gourmet food emporium in 1899. The founders were such sticklers for detail that they had a discreet window inserted in the managers' quarters so that Mr Lewis could keep an eye on the shop floor.

produce to international specialities, so the finest York ham and Cropwell Bishop Stilton are found alongside superb Chatka crab, Russian Stilton and Italian salami. UK delivery with express option.

Mortimer & Bennett
www.mortimerandbennett. co.uk

This delicatessen and online store is crammed full of fine foods from around the world. Many of its food suppliers are small or family-run concerns that make items not available in supermarkets. You'll find an extensive range of cheeses, breads, oils and charcuterie, as well as a selection of fun gifts for 'foodies', such as the La Maison du Miel honey, Italian flower jellies and gold and silver buttons. UK delivery; express option.

The Heavenly Hamper Company
www.theheavenlyhamper-company.co.uk

The aim of Heavenly Hampers is to offer food and wine gifts that you won't find anywhere else. The collection isn't huge, but they've definitely found some interesting products to include, such as red chilli jelly,

aubergines stuffed with anchovies, and onions marinated in balsamic vinegar. UK delivery; express option.

Valvona & Crolla
www.valvonacrolla-online. co.uk

Scotland's oldest delicatessen and Italian wine merchant has been trading since 1934. They offer an excellent range of gourmet Italian products, plus a selection of good-value and decent-quality wines from artisan producers and progressive cooperatives. They also provide an excellent selection of reasonably pricd, pre-packed foods and wine gift suggestions. UK and Ireland delivery.

Virginia Hayward
www.virginiahayward.com

Virginia Hayward runs her business from Shaftesbury in Dorset. She offers a beautifully presented range of traditional gifts and hampers, including the Duchy Originals range. There are gift suggestions of fine food and wine for all

HAMPER HISTORY

The word 'hamper' derives from the old French *hanapier*, meaning 'a case for holding goblets'.

Hampers are an offshoot of the old Boxing Day tradition, when employers would give their servants wicker boxes of useful items on the day after Christmas.

In Victorian times hampers went upmarket and became popular at events such as Henley Regatta and Ascot Races. Fortnum & Mason made their name by providing luxury hampers to the English aristocracy.

seasons and events, from birthdays to weddings, plus romantic gifts, such as flowers and chocolates. Personalised greeting option available. Next-day delivery in UK.

Whisk Hampers
www.whiskhampers.co.uk
The stylish, modern gifts at Whisk are strikingly packaged with a postcard featuring a quotation based on the gift contents. Your personalised message is also included. Choose from an excellent range of champagnes and wines, plus hampers with names such as Dressing to Impress, Kitchen Confidential and Instant Karma. Express UK delivery and gift wrapping.

Whittard of Chelsea
www.whittard.co.uk
Famous for fine tea and coffee since 1886, Whittard's offers a wide range from around the world, including Monsoon Malabar, Old Brown Java and Very Very Berry Fruit Infusion. They also offer instant flavoured cappuccinos, their own hot chocolate, coffee-making equipment, coffee and tea gift sets and colourful ceramics. Ships worldwide; express UK delivery and gift wrapping.

LAST-MINUTE LIFE-SAVERS

I'm going to be completely honest with you here (which I may regret), and tell you that despite all my good advice about the importance of allowing enough time to choose and take delivery of gifts, I am as capable as the next person of leaving it until the last minute. Oh, yes. Having said that, I always have to hand – well, I would, wouldn't I? – my list of reliable emergency gift retailers. This is to stop me from doing what I hate the most; namely, rushing out to the shops in the middle of trying to do everything else, and choosing the wrong gift because I'm in a hurry. You know the feeling.

So here they are: my personal shopping life-savers. Some offer luxury, others are not so 'luxe' orientated. These are shops where you can find a tremendous choice of products – something to please everyone – then wrap it and send it out on your behalf for speedy delivery. Please don't expect your gift to arrive the next day if you leave it until the late afternoon to place your order: it simply won't happen. If you think you might miss the cut-off time for next-day delivery, phone up to ask; don't just assume you're out of luck. All these retailers will really try to help.

Aspinal of London
www.aspinaloflondon.com
Aspinal specialise in leather gifts and accessories, including jewellery boxes, photo albums, leather journals and books. Each item is hand-made by a skilled craftsman, using age-old traditional leather and bookbinding skills. There's a wide choice of colours for all the items and enchanting baby gift ideas as well. Worldwide delivery by courier.

Astley Clarke
www.astleyclarke.com
Luxury online jewellery boutique Astley Clarke sells exquisite contemporary, fine and

> *'You cannot escape the responsibility of tomorrow by evading it today.'*
>
> ABRAHAM LINCOLN

designer jewellery collections from all over the world on an exclusive basis. This is the perfect place to find romantic jewellery gifts or something special for your own enjoyment. All the jewellery is beautifully packaged. Ships worldwide; next-day delivery in the UK.

Bombay Duck
www.bombayduck.co.uk

This is a very pretty home gifts and interiors online retailer with a wide range of ideas, from their own beautifully packaged candles to candy-coloured leather accessories, crystal chandeliers, vintage-style bathroom accessories and printed cushions. Ships worldwide; express delivery option and gift wrapping.

Fortnum & Mason
www.fortnumandmason. com

Here you can buy and order their gorgeously packaged teas, coffees, chocolates, hampers and deli products such as caviar and cheese, dip into their extensive wine cellar and visit their At Home department, which is full of lovely gift ideas and home decor items. Ships worldwide; express UK delivery, and gift wrapping for some items.

Forzieri
www.forzieri.com

Quintessentially Italian, Forzieri has a truly marvellous range of designer footwear, handbags, small leather goods, jewellery and watches, with one of the best collections of leather and shearling coats and jackets you can find anywhere. Ships worldwide; express UK delivery and gift wrapping.

Graham & Green
www.grahamandgreen. co.uk

Graham & Green is a long-established retailer of home and lifestyle products, including candles, tableware, pretty etched glasses, silk cushions, duvet covers and quilts. Founded by friends in 1974, the shop is still in the 'family'. Among their bestsellers are bevelled mirrors, Chinese lanterns and lavender-scented bags. Express UK delivery.

Fortnum & Mason: Grocers to Royalty

❖ Hugh Mason was running a small shop in when he first met William Fortnum in 1705. William was a footman to Queen Anne and a lodger in the Mason's home. Their food emporium expanded rapidly during the Georgian boom years, and they have been known as purveyors of fine teas and other goods ever since.

❖ Every ship that left for the Crimean War during 1815 had on board a Fortnum & Mason hamper of beef tea destined for Florence Nightingale.

❖ In 1886 Fortnum & Mason bought the first consignment of tinned baked beans from a young Mr Heinz.

❖ The famous Fortnum's clock has sixteen bells that have rung every fifteen minutes since 1964.

HQ Man
www.hqman.com

This is an excellent online retailer for men, where you can check out brands such as 4V00, Anthony Logistics, Calmia, Decleor Men, Malin+Goetz, Comptoir-sud-Pacifique and Fred Bennett, and expect to find the full ranges across body, bath, skincare, haircare and accessories. Good service and speedy delivery are the norm here, and they offer gift wrapping as well.

Imogen Stone
www.imogenstone.co.uk

Imogen Stone is a luxury online florist and gift store with a beautifully photographed website. Items on offer include delightful hand-tied bouquets, postal flowers from just £10, and a range of seasonal plants. You can include Rococo chocolate truffles, Abahna toiletries and LSA vases with your order if you wish. Call before 1 p.m. for same-day UK delivery.

I Want One of Those
www.iwantoneofthose.com

This is an irresistible online gift and gadget shop with a huge choice and a very well-designed website. Search by price or product type – you'll find there's a wide range of

*'My fairest, my espoused, my latest found,
Heaven's last best gift, my ever new delight.'*
JOHN MILTON, *PARADISE LOST*

both. The excellent animation for most products makes it easy to select gadgets for garden, kitchen or office, and there are the inevitable toys and games. Ships worldwide; express UK delivery and gift wrapping.

John Lewis
www.johnlewis.com
John Lewis has, without doubt, created the best department store online. It offers a huge range of products, most of which can be delivered within the UK by express delivery, but there is no gift wrapping service. At special times, such as Easter and Christmas, it's advisable to order early as they do sell out of core items. They also have a gorgeous selection of flowers that can be delivered on the date you specify. Over and over again John Lewis proves itself to be the star of stores.

Jo Malone
www.jomalone.co.uk
Jo Malone has a perfect range of fragrances, scented candles, bath and body products, travel 'must-haves' and facial 'fin-ishers'. When choosing a gift here, it is pointless to resist buying something for yourself as well – it's almost impossible. The service is excellent and everything is exquisitely pack-aged in her signature cream and black. Ships worldwide; express UK delivery.

K J Beckett
www.kjbeckett.com
The Beckett brothers set out to become retailers who offer quality and imaginative acces-sories for men – and they have succeeded. They have a really good selection of fashionable and luxury items, including Re-gent belts, cufflinks by Simon Carter, Ian Flaherty and Ver-itas, silk ties, cummerbunds, wallets and handkerchiefs. Ex-press worldwide delivery. UK standard delivery is free, and they'll gift wrap.

Net-a-Porter
www.net-a-porter.com
As the ultimate online fashion retailer, Net-a-Porter might not be the first place you think of for gifts. However, their ac-cessories section offers lots of

possibilities, from fashion jewellery by Me & Ro, Kenneth Jay Lane and Erickson Beamon to scarves by Burberry, Pucci and Chloe, and must-have small leather items. The website resembles a fashion magazine and is a joy to browse. Ships worldwide; express UK delivery and gift wrapping.

Objects of Design
www.objects-of-design.com
Here you'll find gift and home accessory ideas that are all designed and made in Britain, such as Emily Readett-Bayley bookends, wonderful Irish linen by Ferguson, and crystal stemware from Phil Atrill – and that's just to give you an idea. Ships worldwide; express UK delivery and gift wrapping.

Thank Heaven for Chocolate
www.thankheavenforchocolate.co.uk
Here are decorative chocolate hampers, superior Belgian chocolates, gorgeous chocs for Valentine's Day, hand-made truffles, and cute chocolate novelties, such as Saddleback Piglets and Happy Ducks. The selection isn't huge, but is very well thought-out. UK delivery and gift wrapping.

'Rich gifts wax poor when givers prove unkind.'

WILLIAM SHAKESPEARE,
HAMLET

The Baby
www.thebaby.co.uk
This is a gorgeous baby website, offering so much that you could get totally lost in it. Bypass the essential equipment pages and go straight to Getting Dressed, Sleep Me, Care for Me, or Treat Me. You're sure to find the perfect gift. Ships worldwide; express UK delivery and gift wrapping.

The Garden Pharmacy
www.garden.co.uk
This long-established Covent Garden store sells top brands Chanel, Elizabeth Arden, Lancôme, Revlon, Clinique, Clarins, Vichy, Avene, Caudalie and Roc, as well as spa products by I Coloniali, L'Occitane, Roger et Gallet and Segreti Mediterranei. They also offer a huge range of fragrances. Next-day UK delivery and free gift wrapping.

The Toy Shop

www.thetoyshop.com

If it's toys and games you're looking for, this is your one-stop shop. 'More toys, more value and more fun' is their motto, and here you can search by brand, type of toy, age group or price. The range includes Baby Annabel, Dr Who, Hornby, Mattel, Nintendogs and Playmobil, plus a wealth of other popular choices. Ships worldwide; express UK delivery at a standard charge.

The White Company

www.thewhitecompany. com

This is one of my favourite retailers, offering beautiful and stylish products for every room in your house. Choose from lovely bedlinen and quilts, fluffy towels, stunning table lamps, wonderful toiletries, pretty home accessories, baby gifts and lots more. There are great present ideas for everyone. Ships worldwide; express UK delivery.

SPECIAL OCCASION REMINDER SERVICES

Forget about having to put all your special dates in your diary or into a list and updating it each year; or worrying that you will forget someone or something special. Just sign up to a reminder service at one of the websites below. You simply input all the dates you want to remember and tell them how much in advance you'd like to be reminded. Then all you need to do is wait for that reminder email to appear and take action.

All these sites work in the same way, and all will try to sell you cards, balloons and gifts. However, you can choose to use only the free reminder service; whether you do anything else is totally up to you.

www.moonpig.com
www.reminderspot.com
www.thecardandgiftcompany.co.uk

TRAVEL, EVENT TICKETS AND RESTAURANTS

This section gives you my recommendations for the easiest ways of finding and booking places to visit, places to eat, and ways to travel. Most travel arrangements are now arranged online, so the next time you want to book, say, a surprise trip to Morocco, a flight to Paris, or a quick visit to Brussels via Eurostar use this section to make your life easy. Your first choices should probably be www.expedia.co.uk, www.lastminute.com or www.travelocity.co.uk. There you can find just about everything you need. However, take a look below at some other options too, many of which have been well tried and tested by yours truly. There are lots of different guides around, but these, to my mind, are very much the best.

RESTAURANTS AND HOTELS
Michelin
www.viamichelin.co.uk

For the best restaurants anywhere in Europe the Michelin website is the optimum place to start your search, provided of course your choice has managed to make it into the famous Red Guide. Just enter your location into the search box and a list of the closest restaurants and hotels appears, showing the appropriate number of stars or the knife and fork ratings. I trust Michelin and their ratings, and use this site all the time when I'm away.

Top Table
www.toptable.co.uk

Whether you're in New York, London, Paris, Barcelona or any other major city listed on this site, Top Table will provide up-to-the-minute restaurant recommendations. They also tell you the 'hot' places to eat, were to go for special offers and will make your booking. They can organise parties or private dining as well.

Frommer's
www.frommers.com
The Frommer's guides give you the lowdown on a huge range of locations around the world. They will tell you what's going on, where to stay and where to eat almost anywhere you want to go. They are useful for the USA in particular, which is where many of the guides originate; but the UK publisher has recently launched day-by-day guides too. This series is the one I choose every time.

EVENT TICKETS
Aloud.com
www.aloud.com
Aloud sells tickets from Ticketmaster and Ticketweb. It specialises in rock and pop concert tickets, and the alphabetic index in the left-hand column on the homepage allows you to choose quickly from its Hot New Tickets or Best Seller collections. You can book from the UK or internationally.

See
www.seetickets.com
Whether you want to see X Factor Live, Billy Elliot on stage, or Bryn Terfel at Christmas, you can book it here. In fact, you can get tickets for just about anything here, including the Good Food Show, the Clothes Show Live and Horse of the Year show You can also book for events in other countries, such as motoring Grand Prix. They also suggest places to stay.

Ticketmaster
www.ticketmaster.co.uk
Music, theatre and sport tickets are available on this, the original ticket website. If you want standing-room tickets to see Robbie Williams, seats for England vs. Barbarians at Twickenham, a booking for fireworks and music at Hampton Court, or tickets for pretty much anything else, this is your site.

GENERAL TRAVEL
The following sites are extremely good:
www.expedia.co.uk or .com
www.lastminute.com
www.travelocity.co.uk or .com
www.ebookers.com

And specifically try these:
www.eurostar.com
www.eurotunnel.com
www.railbookers.com
for great Eurostar inclusive breaks with special offers.

LIFE'S LITTLE LUXURIES

I'm sure you'll agree with me that everyone needs a little bit of luxury in life. No matter how small or large the gift, just about anything from the stores listed here will bring a bit of sparkle to whoever's receiving it. 'Oh, just a teeny Gucci gift voucher would be so great,' I have often said to my family (to no effect, I might add). But I really mean it, because the brand, with all its luxurious connotations, has such a wonderful warm feeling about it. I know perfectly well why my request is never granted, and it's quite simply because 'teeny' and 'Gucci' do not go together! I'd almost certainly spend more than my allotted amount. However, if you're thinking of giving someone a gift or gift voucher, remember that it's their choice to spend over and above the scope of your generosity. The practicality is that they'll be overjoyed that you have such wonderful taste, even before they've opened the box.

Which leads me on to another point: all the retailers in this section spend a huge amount on their packaging, so forget gift wrapping. Everything they sell is all about beautiful and over-the-top presentation. They say that the best things come in small packages, and I agree. A small package from any of these stores will definitely bring a smile.

Christian Dior
www.dior.com
The name Christian Dior has wowed the world since the 1940s. The online boutique offers its range of covetable handbags, shoes and boots, small leather accessories, scarves, watches and fine jewellery. Prices are steep, but if you want your nearest and dearest to be carrying the latest handbag on her arm this season, you'll no doubt be prepared. Expect speedy shipping and gorgeous packaging.

Dalvey

www.dalvey.com

Dalvey of Scotland has created a range of elegant and useful gifts, which are attractively displayed on their extremely well laid-out website. Items such as beautifully made leather travel clocks and business card cases, cufflinks and cufflink cases, hip flasks and binoculars are all luxuriously presented. Worldwide delivery.

Dunhill

www.dunhill.com

Dunhill is one of the leading designers of English luxury accessories for men, and here you can choose from their range of luggage, briefcases, wash-bags, wallets, diaries, belts, ties and cufflinks. Ships worldwide; speedy delivery and superb packaging.

Fortnum & Mason

www.fortnumand mason. com

At Fortnum & Mason you can buy and order their gorgeously packaged teas, coffees, chocolates, hampers and deli

Definition of luxury:

Something that is inessential but conducive to pleasure and comfort.

products, such as caviar and cheese, dip into their extensive wine cellar and visit their At Home department, which is packed full of lovely gift ideas and home decor items. Ships worldwide; express UK delivery, and gift packaging for some items.

Gucci

www.gucci.com

At Gucci's beautiful online store you can buy handbags, luggage, men and women's shoes, jewellery, sunglasses and gifts such as keyrings and lighters. Everything is very special and beautiful, and you'll be a huge success whatever you buy (provided it can be changed if you've got it wrong). The packaging is gorgeous and they offer express delivery.

Guccio Gucci worked at the Savoy Hotel in London for many years before starting his leather goods company. He opened his first store in his native Florence in 1921.

'My mother says that when I was little my grandfather used to take me and my cousins on one side after dinner and ask us what we wanted to be when we grew up, and I'd say "Christian Dior".'

CHRISTIAN LACROIX

Harrods

www.harrods.com

There is only one Harrods, and it has always been a favourite shopping destination of mine. It is a wonderful store in a beautiful building, and simply bursting with famous name products. On its website you can buy silver and glass, home accessories, food and drink, fashion, handbags, cosmetics and gorgeous bath and body products. Worldwide delivery.

Janet Reger

www.janetreger.com

In her shops and on her beautiful dark website, Janet Reger offers the most gorgeous selection of lingerie, but the prices are not for the faint-hearted. This brand is totally about luxury and glamour, so be prepared to spend a small fortune, but on wonderful quality and style. Ships worldwide; express option and gift wrapping.

Jimmy Choo

www.jimmychoo.com

This is always a totally covetable collection, and currently includes diamanté-encrusted sandals, killer heel peep-toe slides, gorgeous boots and spot-on handbags.Whether you choose to buy in the stores or online, you can expect to come away with something totally of the moment and, in most cases, frighteningly expensive. Ships worldwide with gift presentation.

Linley

www.davidlinley.com

As you would expect, everything from the workshop of David Linley is really beautiful and would make a perfect gift. Furniture is designed and made using traditional techniques and expert craftsmanship. The shop also produces frames, vases, lamps, candlesticks and jewellery boxes, and sells accessories such as home fragrances and cushions. The photographs on the website are really beautiful, so be careful: you'll be spending more than you intended in a nanosecond. Ships worldwide; express UK delivery.

Louis Vuitton
www.louisvuitton.com

Louis Vuitton's unmistakable (and luxuriously expensive) handbags are now available online. Although it's not quite the same experience as buying from the store, the website offers a wealth of information in a readily accessible way. You'll find luggage, briefcases, diaries, sunglasses and watches here. Custom-made goods are available. Worldwide delivery.

Longmire
www.longmire.co.uk

At Longmire you'll find what is probably the best selection of luxury cufflinks available anywhere. Their signature enamel and gold designs cost over £1000, while their art deco-inspired 18ct gold 'stirrup' links are over £2000 (not to mention the black and white diamond revolver cufflinks, which will set you back £5000). Ships worldwide; express option.

Lulu Guinness
www.luluguinness.com

'Be a glamour girl, put on your lipstick' exhorts this elegant website, from which unique, quirky and exquisite handbags and accessories from famous British designer Lulu Guinness can now be shipped to you wherever you are. All goods are gift wrapped in tissue and ribbon in a special Lulu Guinness bag.

Mikimoto
www.mikimoto-store.co.uk

Mikimoto is a name synonymous with beautiful and luxurious pearls, and now you can buy a selection of their bestselling jewellery online as well as in their stores. Prices start at around £120 for a pair of timeless pearl studs and go up to around £2000 for their Tahitian pearl and pink sapphire

'You sold your soul to the devil when you put on your first pair of Jimmy Choos; I saw it.'

EMILY BLUNT TO ANDY SACHS
IN *THE DEVIL WEARS PRADA*

pendants and earrings. Ships worldwide; express UK delivery and gift wrapping.

Pickett
www.pickett.co.uk

Gloves, wallets, briefcases, handbags, belts, umbrellas and stud boxes are just some of the high-quality and beautifully made accessories available at Pickett. If you've ever visited one of their shops, you'll know that everything is the best you can buy, and most items would make lovely gifts, particularly in their deep green boxes tied with orange ribbon. Call them for helpful, friendly advice. Ships worldwide; express UK delivery and gift wrapping.

Smythson
www.smythson.com

Smythson, situated in fashionable Bond Street in central London, has been in business for over a century, selling top-quality personalised stationery and accessories, including diaries, leather journals, albums,

'The saddest thing I can imagine is to get used to luxury.'

CHARLIE CHAPLIN

frames and gold-edged place cards. They now offer covetable handbags and small leather goods in wonderful colours as well. Ships worldwide; express UK delivery and gift wrapping.

Swaine Adeney
www.swaineadeney.co.uk

This company, established in 1750, is well known as a purveyor of the highest-quality gentlemen's accessories, such as umbrellas with unique handles, wallets, attaché and document cases in a variety of styles and leathers, plus wonderful luggage. They have a very good gift selection and many of their items can be personalised. Ships worldwide.

'Give me the luxuries of life, and I will willingly do without its necessities.'

FRANK LLOYD WRIGHT

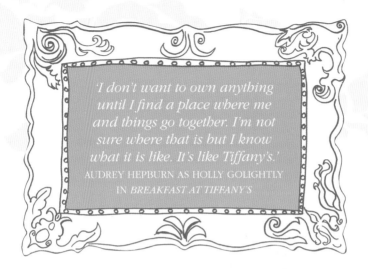

Theo Fennell

www.theofennell.com

Theo Fennell makes beautiful modern jewellery. Among his designs are diamond-studded crosses, horns, hearts and keys, and his solid silver Marmite lids and Worcester sauce-bottle holders, are recognised the world over. Browse the site or visit his store and see if you're tempted. Worldwide delivery.

Tiffany

www.tiffany.com

Anything in the signature Tiffany blue box is sure to make a perfect present, from the smallest piece of Elsa Peretti or Paloma Picasso jewellery to wonderful classic diamonds and pearls. Look for the beautiful Tiffany glass candlesticks, bowls and stemware, the Tiffany fragrance in its lovely glass bottle, and christening gifts for a new baby. Express delivery and automatic gift packaging.

William Evans

www.williamevans.com

Whatever your view of guns and shooting, this traditional gun-maker offers an excellent range of gifts, from shooting-related clothing and accessories to brass-buckled bridle-hide belts, classic leather-strap watches, sterling silver cufflinks, flasks, humidors, lighters and glassware. Worldwide delivery.

DO SOMETHING DIFFERENT –
THINK OUTSIDE THE BOX

While researching this book, I came across more corny ideas for gifts (particularly romantic gestures) than I care to remember, and I'm definitely not going to list them here. Suffice it to say that if you try too hard, you could end up creating the opposite effect to what you intended.

Having said that, you can make some occasions even more special by giving a gift in a unique and surprising way. For example, just after our first son was born, my husband taped a small but very beautiful diamond inside a pretty card. I'll never forget opening it. You might want to try it some time (guys, I hope you're listening to this).

There are lots of things you can do. My family special-ises in surprise parties, particularly for birthdays. The only problem with doing this regularly is that you're always as-suming your six best friends will be turning up for dinner, that food is going to arrive or has already been prepared, or that the reason you haven't heard from those you love is because they've all been asked to keep schtum about some-thing. In fact, they've probably all forgotten/are away/busy. Yes, surprises are great – sometimes.

To do something really different doesn't have to involve spending lots of extra money (although it helps, of course, particularly if you want to take that first-class flight to New York, or stay the weekend at the Ritz), but it does involve lots of extra thought – in advance. Book a table, plan a trip, call a few friends... Make it happen and make it special by finding alternatives to what you normally do for birthdays, anniversaries and other celebrations. Opposite are some ideas to create an occasion that will never be forgotten.

- Arrange a surprise trip anywhere.
- Throw a surprise party (but make sure everyone knows that it's a surprise or your cover will be blown).
- Prepare a photo album, digital or otherwise, containing pictures of friends and family.
- Book a table at a favourite restaurant.
- Find a signed copy, or better still a signed first edition, of a book by a favourite author (visit www.abebooks.com).
- Attach a beautifully wrapped gift voucher or certificate to a token present, such as bath sizzlers for a pampering voucher (www.potions.co.uk) or a serving spoon for an haute cuisine meal (www.culinaryconcepts.co.uk).
- Personalise a label for a champagne bottle (www.next-daychampagne.co.uk or www.barrelsandbottles.co.uk).

NEVER DO THESE

✗ Don't ever take an obviously cheap bottle of wine to someone who serves you the best of everything and allows you to smoke their finest cigars. Better to take a small, beautiful box of chocolates or nothing at all.

✗ Don't give kitchen appliances to your mother; she really won't appreciate them.

✗ Don't give gifts that need assembling unless you're sure that they will be assembled.

✗ Don't give anything that needs to be the right size unless you're absolutely certain you've got the size right. Too small or too large and you might find you're implying something you didn't mean to.

✗ Don't ever buy a gift because it appeals to you rather than the recipient. You will almost certainly be making a mistake.

See also Valentine's Day, page 28.

4 THE GIFT DIARY

THE GIFT DIARY

*T*his part of the book is going to become the most important section for you – it is the place where you can record all the essential dates and pieces of information about the recipients of your gifts that, when brought together, provide everything you need to ensure that your next gift is relevant, amusing, thoughtful, clever. In short – inspired.

Start by filling in the blanks well before you're going to need them. Well before next Christmas; well before that important anniversary or birthday; well before any other gift-giving milestone.

Don't forget to sign up with one of the Special Occasion Reminder Services (see page 223) as well. Reading this book will help you decide what to buy, but it won't ring the alarm when you're about to forget an important date. The reminder service will, so you need that too.

Read 'What makes a present perfect?' on page 10 to help you identify each person's likes and dislikes. These will form the basis of your gift decisions. Then fill in one of the sections in the following pages for each person to whom you regularly give gifts.

Name *The Cotton Patch*

Email *www.Cottonpatch.co.uk*

Address *Clover Felting Needle.*

Postcode

Telephone   Mobile phone

Birthday   Age at entry

Hobbies and interests

Personal style

Lifestyle and home style

Loves, likes and dislikes

Keep track of other valuable information, such as anniversary
dates, partner's name, the names and birth dates of their children,
memorable moments (such as when or where you met), place of
work, date of a house move, nationality, etc.

GIFT LIST

Date   Gift
_____

_____

Date   Gift
_____

_____

Date   Gift
_____

_____

Date   Gift
_____

_____

Date   Gift
_____

_____

Date   Gift
_____

_____

Date   Gift
_____

_____

Date   Gift
_____

_____

Name

Email

Address

                              Postcode

Telephone   Mobile phone

Birthday   Age at entry

Hobbies and interests

Personal style

Lifestyle and home style

Loves, likes and dislikes

Keep track of other valuable information, such as anniversary dates, partner's name, the names and birth dates of their children, memorable moments (such as when or where you met), place of work, date of a house move, nationality, etc.

GIFT LIST

Date   Gift

_____

Date   Gift

_____

Date   Gift

_____

Date   Gift

_____

Date   Gift

_____

Date   Gift

_____

Date   Gift

_____

Date   Gift

_____

Name

Email

Address

Postcode

Telephone   Mobile phone

Birthday   Age at entry

Hobbies and interests

Personal style

Lifestyle and home style

Loves, likes and dislikes

Keep track of other valuable information, such as anniversary
dates, partner's name, the names and birth dates of their children,
memorable moments (such as when or where you met), place of
work, date of a house move, nationality, etc.

GIFT LIST

Date   Gift

Date   Gift

Date   Gift

Date   Gift

Date   Gift

Date   Gift

Date   Gift

Date   Gift

Name _____

Email _____

Address _____

_____ Postcode _____

Telephone _____ Mobile phone _____

Birthday _____ Age at entry _____

Hobbies and interests _____

_____

Personal style _____

Lifestyle and home style _____

Loves, likes and dislikes _____

_____

Keep track of other valuable information, such as anniversary
dates, partner's name, the names and birth dates of their children,
memorable moments (such as when or where you met), place of
work, date of a house move, nationality, etc.

_____

_____

GIFT LIST

Date _____ Gift _____

_____

Date _____ Gift _____

_____

Date _____ Gift _____

_____

Date _____ Gift _____

_____

Date _____ Gift _____

_____

Date _____ Gift _____

_____

Date _____ Gift _____

_____

Date _____ Gift _____

_____

Name _____

Email _____

Address _____

_____ Postcode _____

Telephone _____ Mobile phone _____

Birthday _____ Age at entry _____

Hobbies and interests _____

_____

Personal style _____

Lifestyle and home style _____

Loves, likes and dislikes _____

_____

Keep track of other valuable information, such as anniversary dates, partner's name, the names and birth dates of their children, memorable moments (such as when or where you met), place of work, date of a house move, nationality, etc.

_____

_____

GIFT LIST

Date   Gift

Date   Gift

Date   Gift

Date   Gift

Date   Gift

Date   Gift

Date   Gift

Date   Gift

Name

Email

Address

                       Postcode

Telephone   Mobile phone

Birthday   Age at entry

Hobbies and interests

Personal style

Lifestyle and home style

Loves, likes and dislikes

Keep track of other valuable information, such as anniversary dates, partner's name, the names and birth dates of their children, memorable moments (such as when or where you met), place of work, date of a house move, nationality, etc.

GIFT LIST

Date   Gift

Date   Gift

Date   Gift

Date   Gift

Date   Gift

Date   Gift

Date   Gift

Date   Gift

Name _____

Email _____

Address _____

_____ Postcode _____

Telephone _____ Mobile phone _____

Birthday _____ Age at entry _____

Hobbies and interests _____

_____

Personal style _____

Lifestyle and home style _____

Loves, likes and dislikes _____

_____

Keep track of other valuable information, such as anniversary dates, partner's name, the names and birth dates of their children, memorable moments (such as when or where you met), place of work, date of a house move, nationality, etc.

_____

_____

GIFT LIST

Date   Gift

Date   Gift

Date   Gift

Date   Gift

Date   Gift

Date   Gift

Date   Gift

Date   Gift

A GRACIOUS
THANK YOU

*T*hanking people personally for thoughtful acts and gifts is essential. Forget to do so and you will always be remembered as the one who couldn't be bothered. Remember, and thank beautifully, and it will be really appreciated, particularly as present-day informality means that many people don't thank properly.

Here are a few tips

✿ Thank as quickly as possible, and refer directly to the gift or act that has led you to write. 'Thank you for your lovely gift' on its own just won't do – sorry.

✿ For special thanks, such as after you've been taken out for a smart lunch or dinner, or to the theatre, and where you'd like to do more than just write a note, consider sending flowers, chocolates or something pampering. The presentation is important here: you don't have to spend a fortune (and you definitely shouldn't go over the top), but something small and gorgeous from Jo Malone, a pretty hydrangea in a ceramic pot, or a small selection of luxury chocs will all do well for this type of thanks.

✿ Thank yous by email or phone are fine for people you know really well. For others, take the time to put pen to (high-quality) paper or card. An email to someone you have just met who has done something special for you or given you a gift is not good enough.

ALWAYS THANK FOR THE FOLLOWING:

✿ Wedding gifts
✿ Sympathy letters
✿ Flowers
✿ Baby or bridal shower gifts
✿ Gifts you've received if you've been in hospital
✿ Being a house guest
✿ Gifts received by mail or by hand, whether or not you've already thanked the giver in person
✿ Being a dinner party guest (although it's accepted now to thank by phone if you know your host well)
✿ Any special favour that has been done for you

DON'T DO THESE:

✗ Delay in thanking for more than a week
✗ Send out pre-written thank-you notes – a real no-no for any type of gift
✗ Forget to thank – ever

*'Every gift which is given, even
though it is small, is in reality
great, if it is given with affection.'*

PINDAR (LYRICAL POET OF ANCIENT GREECE)

Vicki — Philosphy — Gingerbread Shower
    coco chanel.   shampoo/
                                    Tell.

Rachel —

ACKNOWLEDGEMENTS

The publishers would like to thank the following for their help in researching and supplying the photographs: Frances Ekiko of Amanda Wakeley Jewels; Iain Burton and Rudy Leander of Aspinal of London; Sally Oxenham of Astley Clarke Jewellery; Kate Byrn of Biscuiteers; James Felton and Nikki of Butler and Wilson; Emma Chapman of Emma Chapman Jewels; Anita of For Goodness Cakes; Clare Hutchison and Simon Evans of FrouFrou and Thomas; Ellen Westbrook and Janet Bradley at The Goodwood Motor Circuit; Mark Walker of Ice Cool; Emma Brannan of Jojo Maman Bebe; Paul Balland of JW Flowers; Karen Berman of Karen Berman PR; Lyn Joseph of Lyn Joseph PR; Anton Pruden of Pruden & Smith; Karen Watson and her team at The Real Flower Company; Olivia and Clara of The Ribbon Shop; Carolyn Dunster of Simply Roses.

Permissions

Photographs have been reproduced with the kind permission of the following copyright holders:
page 18 Royal Old Gold and page 236 Sheer Elegance Aubergine © The Ribbon Shop; page 28 Pearl Queen heart necklace with citrine, garnet and pearls © Full Focus photography, supplied by Emma Chapman; page 40 Summer white, Mother's Day bouquet © The Real Flower Company; page 50 Betty's Easter egg © Bettys-by-Post at Betty's and Taylors of Harrogate; page 56 Lewis Hamilton at the Goodwood Revival © John Colley, supplied by The Goodwood Motor Circuit; page 66 Silk mikado panelled dress from Sposa, Rajastan collection © Amanda Wakeley; page 80 L.O.V.E. spells love tin © Biscuiteer Baking Company; page 88 Dolls House Bookcase (48 x 70 x 20cm) © Jojo Maman Bebe; page 96 Dedalo platinum vase © Versace; supplied by dotmaison, with the kind permission of Versace; page 102 Christmas crackers – boxed set © Froufrou and Thomas; page 254 Rosebuds pomander © Simply Roses. The background wallpapers used throughout the book are copyright © Shutterstock.com and have been reproduced with their permission.

Poems: p125 'Denbigh Boy Racer' © Gareth Glyn Roberts; p. 163 Extract from 'Prayer of a sportsman' © Berton Braley Cyber Museum www.bertonbraley.com. p.51 © Charles M. Shultz **Extracts:** p. 174 'Two ways to get in shape to own a horse' adaptedfromhexbomb-at-blogspot.blogspot.com/2007/01/ten-ways-to-get-in-shape-to-own-a-horse.html; p.168 © Michael Green, The art of coarse sailing, Robson Books, 1988; p.103 © Clement C. Moore, 'A visit from St Nicholas' (Houghton Mifflin, 2005). **Quotes:** p.149 www.agallery.com; pp.67, 75, 116, 120, 127, 139, 161, 172 www.brainyquote.com; p.179 www.croquetworld.com; p.176 www.creativequotations.com; p.42 www.dayformothers.com; p.146 www.famousquotes.com; p.196 www.fragranceonline.com; pp.132, 133 www.gingerrogers.com; p.116 www.quotationsbook.com; pp.156, 183 www.quotationspage.com; pp.49, 60, 74, 120, 136, 147, 148, 180, 193, 205, 216 www.thinkexist.com; p.105 © Twentieth Century Fox.

ABOUT THE AUTHOR

After twelve years of selling international designer fashion by mail order, Patricia Davidson started www.thesiteguide.com, the online luxury fashion, beauty and lifestyle website directory described as 'the web's best shopping directory' by Condé Nast's Glamour.com.

She has written six books about online shopping. Her first, *The Shopaholic's Guide to Buying Online*, was published by Capstone in October 2006. She has also written features for magazines and newspapers, and been interviewed for television and radio. Described by Eamonn Holmes as 'the fairy godmother of online shopping', she lives in Buckinghamshire with her husband, three children and two dogs.

AUTHOR'S ACKNOWLEDGEMENTS

My thanks to everyone at John Wiley (Capstone) – Jason Dunne, Emma Swaisland, Julia Lampam, Katie Moffat, Iain Campbell, Megan Varilly, Grace O'Byrne and Jenny Ng – for their faith in asking me to write this book and their enthusiasm and commitment to making it a success. Particular thanks go to Sarah Sutton, Annette Peppis and Trish Burgess, for taking my scruffy manuscript and, with enormous dedication, turning it into this gorgeously designed book.

Jonny Geller is the agent every author wants to have, and I'd like to thank him, Doug Keane and Alice Lutyens at Curtis Brown for their continued help and support. Thanks also to Lee, Chris and Simon of E2E Solutions for their great work on and help with my website.